T0328344

"Gil Crosby has accomplished what most of us in the world of applied behavioral science, in general, and OD and T-Group training, in particular, have not—making the theoretical father of our work accessible. Thus, this book is a gift and with it we can understand more deeply and teach others more accurately what Lewin actually stated and meant. Moreover, the book is reader-friendly, visually appealing, and humorous rather than academically boring. Thank you, Gil!"

Dr. W. Warner Burke
E.L. Thorndike Professor of Psychology and Education
Teachers College, Columbia University

"Students and practitioners of Organization Development will find this analysis of Lewin's theories and models very helpful both to understand better how this brilliant mind worked and to see how his theories of change led both to seminal research and to the training of several generations of consultants. Much of what we take for granted was first formulated by Lewin and his students, and much of our practice of experiential learning such as the use of group dynamics and the T-group evolved directly out of Lewin's models. This book is both important history and a useful statement of change theory and practice."

Edgar Schein
Professor Emeritus, MIT
Author with son Peter of *Humble Leadership* (2018) and
the third edition of *The Corporate Culture Survival Guide* (2019)

"Kurt Lewin's insights were the starting point for a school of thought that has been immensely influential. Without the practice he engendered, our organizations – and our world – would run amok. Two hours with this book will bring you up to speed."

Art Kleiner, author, *The Age of Heretics*

"Lewin was one of the great psychologists of the 20th century, but today much of his work has been forgotten or misunderstood. This well-written and well-researched book introduces us to Lewin the man, Lewin the scholar and Lewin the practitioner. It not only illustrates the depth of his work, but also the humanitarian values on which it was built. Above all, it demonstrates the continuing relevance of Lewin's work and the concerns that drove it. Gil Crosby has produced a great book and I very much look forward to buying it and recommending it to colleagues and students."

Bernard Burnes
Chair of Organisational Change, Stirling Management School
University of Stirling, Scotland

"I have used Crosby's coaching for over two decades, and it has consistently paid off for me personally and for the teams and organizations I have led. I strongly endorse this book for anyone in a leadership position, whether they are just starting out or are in an executive-level position and deep into their career. There is a science behind organization effectiveness, and that science is made clear in this book. The guidance and insights regarding change and leadership are invaluable."

Senior Utility Executive

"Congratulations Gil on your composing an astute, thorough, and timely analysis of Kurt Lewin's creative contributions to applied social psychology. I especially appreciate your Chapter 8 on education and how beautifully you celebrate your father's ways of building on the Lewin legacy in the later chapters. I hope that this significant and well-written manuscript will inspire readers to return to the seminal works of the master."

Dick Schmuck
Professor Emeritus, University of Oregon

"Meeting Gil Crosby was a pivotal moment in my life. A moment that would lead me on a journey to change my approach to group dynamics. I gained knowledge that greatly enhanced my ability to work and achieve goals with others. Before meeting Gil I would describe my approach to group dynamics as helter-skelter at best! I would insert my personal emotions into every situation. Some things just don't merit an emotional response; they just merit process! Good luck my friend...this is a good read!"

Pat Roberson
Ret. United Steel Workers, VP local 9448

"Gil Crosby has written a must-read primer for anyone considering sustainable organisational change and improvement, while at the same time taking us back to the basics of social science through a thorough understanding of Kurt Lewin's principles of planned change. The most fundamental learnings in my career about how to effect change, what leadership is and how social dynamics and 'T-groups' can unlock an organisation's potential came from Gil's organisation. Read this book...and learn from one of the best."

Bridget McCall
Business Improvement Manager, Kestrel Coal

"Gilmore Crosby has provided more than the technical and practical understanding one needs to appreciate and apply my grandfather's ideas in this book. Crosby has also captured the heart, the values, and the high respect for the individual that drove all of Kurt Lewin's work. I am glad he is continuing to share and pass along this valuable insight about Lewin's legacy, which is needed as much now as anytime since his death."

Michael Papanek
Leadership and OD Consultant, Grandson of Kurt Lewin

"This book is a rich, thoughtful and accessible integration of Kurt Lewin's theoretical framework of change theory and the many applications to organizations, communities and practice. Kurt Lewin's life's work has been foundational to my professional practice as an organization development and leadership consultant, faculty and writer. It is an essential foundation for anyone who seeks to integrate the individual, group/team, organizational, and societal levels. Gil Crosby has made this treasure trove accessible and engaging with his storytelling style and the focus of the many applications including social justice, group process and planned change."

Ilene C. Wasserman, Ph.D.
President, ICW Consulting Group
Board Member –The Lewin Center
Senior Leadership Fellow, Executive Coach and Learning
Director, McNulty Leadership Program /Wharton School /
The University of Pennsylvania
Faculty, PCOM Medical College School of Psychology

"Gil's new book peels the onion back on the methods he used during our long and fruitful collaboration. This exploration of Kurt Lewin's planned change methods teaches eye opening lessons and provides a reliable path to high productivity and results. The only reason to not follow these methods is a lack of awareness that they exist. This book will hopefully eliminate that excuse. The book is an easy read that provides clarity on how to change individuals, groups, organizations, and even societies. It shows the potential of democratic leadership, and the folly of authoritarian and passive leadership styles. Companies should use it to create effective groups and leaders at all levels within their organization!"

Jerome Maxwell
Former Managing Director, Jamalco Alumina Refinery

"I'm glad Gil Crosby decided to write this piece. I have been using the principles taught by Lewin for over 18 years during my Operations Management journey in the mining and chemical world. Cotton and Gil did a nice job at communicating how Lewin principles applied to the workplace and how this information applied to our personal improvement. I have been a part and a witness of amazing culture transformation in organizations due to the discovery of this information by every individual that participated. It is up to us now to continue to practice the knowledge developed by Lewin, adapt it to our own realities, and enjoy the benefits of engaging the entire organization."

David Ledesma
Plant Manager, DuPont – Buffalo NY

"Reading Gil's book left me with the feeling of sorrow that our field no longer produces giants to take the next steps forward in our rapidly changing world. The next steps forward must be grounded in the intent and context of what the founder father Lewin was all about—and no one does this better than Gil."

Allon Shevat
OD Professional, Tel Aviv

"This book provides a well written overview to the life, theories and impact of Kurt Lewin, the social psychologist who catalyzed the study of group dynamics and the creation of democratic, re-educative processes for organizational and social change."

Gervase Bushe
Professor of Leadership and Organization Development
Simon Fraser University, Vancouver, Canada

"Occasionally an extraordinary person steps out of accepted thought and takes a new path—illuminating a new reality; new truths; new methods. Psychoanalytic thought was dominant when Kurt Lewin's theory essentially said, Wake up! Look! What's going on now was not all caused from the past. Pow! New vision. New territory. New methods. We now see the importance of relationships, small groups and interactions as a focus for social change, rather than personal typologies or personalities. Gil's book is a wonderful introduction to Kurt Lewin's motivation, his theory and current examples of what his thought has stimulated. It is a 'Must-Read' for organizational change agents. Thank you Gil."

Ron Short, Ph.D.
Author of *A Special Kind of Leadership*

"Gil's arduous curation of the history of Lewin is a supreme service. The movement from Lewinian precepts to the granular detail of Lewin's own personal values and struggles grips the reader in primal delight. Gil ably demystifies the origins of action research and organization development with delectable placement of events and their significance to the impact Lewin had on them.

The anthropological, sociological, psychological and political history of Lewin's life-history make for rich multidisciplinary evidencing, right through the book. It will likely restore the role of science in OD at a time when the action bias has distorted practice. The pristine quality of Lewin's work as process of inquiry is the book's welcome relief from the anxious excess on outcomes in our lives.

This rare work makes for the Gestalt that the hurried OD practitioner has missed or at best paid lip service to."

Joseph George Anjilvelil
Founder, Workplace Catalysts LLP, Bangalore, India
Author of *BEING PEOPLE : Life-histories of Six HRD Professionals of India*

"Kurt Lewin was a pioneer in the theory and practice of organizational development, but his life and work are not well known. Gilmore Crosby has done our field a great service by writing this well-researched and accessible book."

Adam Kahane
Author of *Power and Love, Solving Tough Problems*
& *Collaborating with the Enemy*

"As a social worker and chief executive of a non-profit human services agency, I grew into an accidental OD professional. Learning from contemporary researchers and a variety of consultants, including Gil Crosby, I increasingly designed and implemented cultural interventions to help the organization achieve aspirational goals for youth. What a difference this book could have made earlier in my career! *Planned Change* provides an overview of Kurt Lewin's research and theories of group process and organizational change. With just a little bit of imagination, I could see the connections between this grandfather of organization development work and current initiatives in schools and work places to address emotional intelligence and build agency in individuals and groups. I recommend this book for any organizational leader as an important introduction to this modern social scientist's work, foundational to our developing efforts to support powerful and effective individual and group performance."

Janis Avery
Retired Non-Profit CEO

"I have known Gil Crosby since the 1970s and have watched him mature into an extraordinary OD professional. Standing on the tall shoulders of 'giants' like Marvin Weisbord, Richard Schmuck, and his father, Robert (Bob) Crosby, Gil has emerged as the foremost authority on the founder of our field, Kurt Lewin. This book, which is an exciting exploration and interpretation of Lewin's writing, proves my case. Well done young Crosby!"

Dr. John J. Scherer
Founding Partner, Scherer Leadership Center
Author, *Facing the Tiger: Five Questions that Change Everything*

"A fresh and very readable, actually enjoyable, book about the Gestalt psychologist who conceptualized social-psychology and thus mightily influenced the lives and practices of many. Certainly OD may not have even existed without this genius who lost his mother in the holocaust. This book highlights how Lewin, an apostle for democracy, is incredibly relevant today. He fled Hitler's ultra-nationalist, xenophobic, anti-semitic fascism. My son Gil has brought Lewin to life in a new way."

Robert P. Crosby
Founder, Crosby & Associates
Leadership Institute of Spokane/Seattle
Author of *Memoirs of a Change Agent: T-groups, Organization Developement, and Social Justice*

Planned Change

Planned Change

Why Kurt Lewin's Social Science is Still Best Practice for Business Results, Change Management, and Human Progress

Gilmore Crosby

CRC Press
Taylor & Francis Group
Boca Raton London New York

CRC Press is an imprint of the
Taylor & Francis Group, an **informa** business

First published 2021
by Routledge
600 Broken Sound Parkway #300, Boca Raton FL, 33487

and by Routledge
2 Park Square, Milton Park, Abingdon, Oxon, OX14 4RN

Routledge is an imprint of the Taylor & Francis Group, an informa business

© 2021 Gilmore Crosby.

The right of Gilmore Crosby to be identified as author of this work has been asserted by him in accordance with sections 77 and 78 of the Copyright, Designs and Patents Act 1988.

Library of Congress Cataloging-in-Publication Data
A catalog record for this title has been requested

ISBN: 978-0-367-53577-3 (hb)
ISBN: 978-0-367-53572-8 (pb)
ISBN: 978-1-003-08249-1 (ebk)

Typeset in Garamond
by Cenveo Publishers Services

Dedication

This text is dedicated to a dear friend and a great Lewinian practitioner, Carey "Cotton" Mears. Cotton not only created his own highly effective version of T-group based learning and action research, he was also a great example of Lewin's strategy and values around transferring knowledge to the people the social scientist was serving.

My father, Robert P. Crosby, lives by that creed. While delivering OD services at an aluminum smelter in Indiana, dad and Cotton, a pot room tender (one of the toughest jobs in the smelter) and union steward, formed a lasting bond. Dad was there training and transferring social science skills to people at all levels of the organization, including Cotton. Cotton loved what he learned and turned it into a new path for himself and many others. RIP Mr. Mears.

Carey "Cotton" Mears: 1956 - 2019

Contents

Acknowledgments

First and foremost, I owe my professional career to the subject of this book, Kurt Lewin. The book itself should be ample testimony to my respect for and debt to this extraordinary man.

My knowledge of Lewin and his methods has come primarily from my father, organization development (OD) practitioner extraordinaire, Robert P. Crosby, and so he gets the second tip of my hat. Dad, by the way, is still sound of mind and engaged in life socially and professionally at 91 at the time of this writing. His latest book, *Memoirs of a Change Agent: T-groups, Organization Development, and Social Justice*, just hit the presses in October 2019. You will get to know him better, especially towards the later end of this book.

From my father, with my mother's help (thanks, Mom!), came my primary professional peer, a skilled OD professional and a scholar in his own right, my brother Chris Crosby. Chris has been a support through thick and thin, which is a rare blessing for an independent consultant to have. And like most brothers, we have had our fair share of conflicts, and are both the better for it. Thanks Chris!

Thanks also to my son Willow, for helping my colleagues and me understand Lewin's formulas, and for helping me get over my fear of topography. I'm proud of his doctorate in physics!

Another deep tip of my hat goes to the plethora of other mentors and colleagues I have been blessed with, including my OD professors John Scherer, Ron Short, Brenda Kerr and Denny Minno, my early OD supervisor Rob Schachter, my step-mother and OD colleague Patricia Crosby, my sub-contractors and peers Cotton Mears, Mark Horswood, and Pam Madison, just to name a few.

I appreciate the respect and support Michael Papanek, the grandson of Kurt Lewin, has given me in this project.

I would know nothing and be making my living some other way if not for my customers, especially Jerome Maxwell, Paul Hinnenkamp, who have pulled on me for decades, and David Ledesma, my current "full speed ahead" collaboration. I've had many other great partnerships along the way, and I am thankful for all of them. A big thank you to the thousands of people in organizations who have given me a chance and helped my interventions succeed.

This book, with its brushing of cultural anthropology, brought me back full circle to my favorite undergraduate professor, Stephanie Coontz. Stephanie took me under her wing when I was a nervous freshman and helped me learn to think systemically and across disciplines. Her objective approach to the social construction of gender roles helped me become more scientific in all of my thinking.

A gigantic tip of the hat to my OD colleague professor Rodney Coates and his co-authors Abby Ferber and David Brunsma for bringing much needed scientific objectivity to the emotionally charged topic of race.

Like my mom's much appreciated contribution of bringing my brother and me into the world (as well as my other siblings, even though they did not follow the OD path), my son Parson ("Par") has taught me a lot as he has become a father and I in turn a grandfather. My grandson, now almost three, is in a photographic example in this text. Mom did a great job of raising us by the way, as my son is also doing. As a father I know that is easier said than done. My grandson gets a tip of the hat for doing a great job of developing!

Every day I give thanks to the Great Spirit from whence we all have come. As my maternal grandfather, Methodist Pastor Lewis Frees used to say every day, in good times and bad, "God is good."

Last but not least, I would be lost without my wife Lisa, who puts up with my hours of writing and my frequent business trips with surprising patience. Like the song says, you, my love, are my motivation.

Introduction

Kurt Lewin (1890-1947) was a visionary psychologist and social scientist who used rigorous research methods to establish an approach to planned change that is both practical and reliable. He mentored and inspired most of the early professionals who came to identify themselves as practitioners of organization development (OD). He also fostered the emergence of the experiential learning method known as the T-group, which uniquely structures group dynamics into a laboratory for dramatic individual and team development. In the early days, most OD professionals learned much about themselves and about group dynamics through T-group experiences.

Lewin's methods, though little known, yield consistent business results such as increased performance and morale. His methods have the rare impact of not just changing behavior, but of changing the beliefs that underlie behavior.

Sadly, most OD professionals today, business and organizational leaders, community organizers, and people in general, have never read any of Lewin's actual writing beyond a quote or two. Indeed, some in the OD profession have rejected or distanced themselves from what they think Lewin taught, even though they and many others seem to know very little about his methods or history.

This problem is not for lack of material. Lewin was a prolific writer. On the other hand, even for someone who deeply admires Lewin, reading his material isn't always easy. His multi-disciplinary approach integrates scientific research methodology, sociology, anthropology, physics, and topography as well as other subjects into an experimental framework that can be overwhelming at a glance. Some of his writing, however, such as *Experiments in Social Space* (Lewin, 1939, 1997, p59-67), is easy enough to understand and apply, and should be a requirement in any OD education.

Although Lewin held a doctorate in psychology and most of his publications are in psychological journals and books, this book is written from the perspective of an organization development practitioner. Having said that, my secondary field is psychiatric social work. In studying for my MSW and for certification to practice I was educated in psychology. That was a long time ago, but I don't recall ever hearing of Lewin during that time. Whether you are familiar with Lewin or not, if you are a psychologist, I hope this kindles your interest in his writing. Although my focus here is on planned change, in Lewin's universal frame work that includes individual change, and absolutely includes psychology.

With that in mind, this book is aimed at introducing Lewin in a new way, both simplified yet substantial enough to guide anyone who is trying to plan change, whether at the individual, group/team, organizational, or societal level.

Lewin often used graphics to illustrate his findings. My hope is that by interspersing them along with other pictures and drawings the concepts will be brought to life in a way that speaks to a wide audience. If it says "Crosby" after a drawing, that one is mine!

A wide audience is important because Lewin was not trying to create methods for OD professionals alone (or for social scientists as he regarded himself). In his interventions he taught everyone he could how to continue to do their own version of planned change. He believed social science might be the light that helps create a brighter future for humanity. I have the same hope. Transferring this knowledge to a broader audience is my intention here, as it has been taught to me by my Lewinian mentor.

I became an OD practitioner in 1984, following in the footsteps of my father, Robert P. Crosby. Dad was in his first T-group in 1953, and was mentored by one of Lewin's primary proteges, Ronald Lippitt, for decades. I had a vague idea that

I was practicing Lewinian OD all these years, but that heritage has become much clearer to me recently, as I became motivated to explore the writings of Lewin in a much more disciplined way. What I have discovered has taught me, an old dog, new tricks. I am determined to spread the wealth.

I have relied heavily on Lewin's writing, organized with the intention of weaving together his thinking in a manner that paints a clear picture for the reader. There are many quotes and citations. Many of Lewin's papers are collected in two wonderful anthologies published by the American Psychological Association (APA). The first, *Resolving Social Conflicts & Field Theory in Social Science*, was published in 1997, the second, *The Complete Social Scientist*, in 1999. To acknowledge these anthologies, I have chosen to cite the original source by year, and add the APA dates and pages (since the two APA books are where most readers are likely to access the material). Hence you will see citations like this throughout this manuscript: (Lewin, 1943, 1997, p___).

Please also note that if a quote runs more than one page, I am only citing the starting page.

I have bolded what I consider to be key phrases and concepts throughout the text, many of which are summarized in Chapter 1. These are identified by the annotation (my bolding).

Most quotes, of course, are in quotation marks. Long passages, such as those with their own heading, are separated from the surrounding text rather than being placed in quotation marks.

My father's approach to Lewinian OD is important to this text. That left me with the awkward choices of either always referring to him by name (as if he were not my father, which is something that I don't actually do), referring to him as father, which is more formal than I prefer, or calling him dad, which is what I actually do. For better or worse, I decided to intermix all three.

Finally, although it may hurt the acceptance of my work by bucking up against established norms of "serious scholarly writing" in some circles, I none-the-less prefer a sense of humor in my reading and have tried to instill it in my writing. I also believe a bit of levity is true to Lewin's character, so as Jimmy Buffet would say, "that is my story and I am sticking to it."

Section I
Lewinian Principles of Planned Change

Kurt Lewin

Chapter 1
Lewinian Principles of Planned Change

Our journey begins at the end—with a summary of Kurt Lewin's principles of planned change. I do so to allow the reader to quickly appraise their value, yet I do so with some trepidation. People have been oversimplifying Lewin's theories and methods since soon after his death, and then dismissing or attacking them as too simple. Please don't make that mistake. That being said, here is my summary of the principles of planned change, followed by explanations of each:

Nine Principles of Lewinian Planned Change

1. **Scientific Methods**
2. **Training—Action—Research**
3. **Group Dynamics**
4. **Democratic Principles and Leadership**
5. **Group Decision**
6. **Change as Three Steps**
7. **Field Theory**
8. **Social Construction of Reality**
9. **Everlasting Change for the Betterment of Humanity**

1. Scientific Methods

As Lewin put it, "There is nothing so practical as a good theory (Lewin, 1943, 1999, p336)." Lewin rigorously applied scientific method to planned change. Because of this his methods can be clearly described and applied to any organizational or social change.

2. Training—Action—Research

The basic elements of planned change included: "...action, research, and training as a triangle (Lewin, 1946, 1997, p149)."

Such training–action–research (as Lewin's student and colleague Dr. Ronald Lippitt more correctly put it in his 1949 book), more commonly referred to as "action research," is to be conducted at multiple levels. Most important to addressing the immediate situation is *participant* action research; action research by the people facing the problem: "The laws (of social science) don't do the job of diagnosis which has to be done locally. Neither do laws prescribe the strategy for change (Lewin, 1946, 1997, p150)."

A corresponding "law of social science" is that solutions are much more likely to be implemented by the people who come up with them. Imposed solutions are likely to flounder. By engaging the people facing the problem, the social scientist is already shifting a potential restraining force (trying to hand off or impose the solution) into a driving force: "It can be surmised that the extent to which social research is translated into social action depends on the degree to which those who carry out this action are made a part of the fact-finding on which the action is to be based (Lewin, 1945, 1997, p55)."

Also important is research by the social scientist so as to continuously test, improve, and add to the body of knowledge on planned change. As Lewin put it, there are: "Two Types of Research Objectives—It is important to understand clearly that social research concerns itself with two rather different types of questions, namely the study of general laws of group life and the diagnosis of a specific situation (Lewin, 1946, 1997, p145)."

3. Group Dynamics

Lewin's research clearly documents that group versus individual interventions prove to be far more effective as a method of planned change: "...it is easier to change ideology or cultural habits by dealing with groups than with individuals (Lewin, 1944, 1999, p289)."

Group dynamics are critical to planned change because individuals are heavily influenced by their primary social environments: "B = f(P,E)–Behavior is a function of the person AND the environment (Lewin, 1940, 1997, p188)."

Group dynamics are the practical doorway into application of all of these principles, and all of these principles are present in group dynamics.

4. Democratic Principles and Leadership

Planned change doesn't happen in a power vacuum. Lewin was clear that understanding, influencing, and working with authority relationships is critical to planned change. He is quoted as saying, "We have to realize that power itself is an essential aspect of any and every group (Marrow, 1969, p172)."

The type of authority that yields the best results is clear: "Democratic Leadership—a group atmosphere can be changed radically in a relatively short time by introducing new leadership techniques...(Lewin, 1944, 1999, p289)."

Democratic leadership involves allowing freedom and influence while still clearly being in charge: "The experiments show that this shift in roles cannot be accomplished by a 'hands off' policy. To apply the principle of 'individualistic freedom' merely leads to chaos...to be able to change a group atmosphere toward democracy the democratic leader has to be in power and has to use his power for active re-education (Lewin, 1943, 1997, p43-45)."

Leadership and followership based on democratic principles takes skills that can't be relied on to come naturally:

"Autocracy is imposed on the individual. Democracy he has to learn (Lewin, 1939, 1997, p66)." "Autocratic and democratic leadership consists of playing a certain role. These roles of the leader cannot be carried through without the followers playing certain complementary roles, namely, those of an autocratic or a democratic follower...The democratic follower has to learn to play a role which implies, among other points, a fair share of responsibility toward the group and a sensitivity to other people's feelings (Lewin, 1944, 1999, p289)."

One of Lewin's most creative inventions was a learning process called the "T-group," in which participants learn democratic principles by applying scientific objectivity to their immediate interactions. We will explore T-groups in depth in Chapters 10 and 12.

5. Group Decision

Effective group involvement in diagnosis and decision shifts group dynamics from being a restraining force to a driving force for change: "The procedure of group decision in this experiment follows a step-by-step method designed (a) to secure high involvement and (b) not to impede freedom of decision (Lewin, 1947, 1999, p271)."

"...complete acceptance of previously rejected facts can be achieved best through the discovery of these facts by the group members themselves (Lewin, 1945, 1997, p55)."

"We have seen that a planned social change may be thought of as composed of unfreezing, change of level, and freezing on the new level. In all three respects group decision has the general advantage of the group procedure (Lewin, 1947, 1997, p331)."

Specifically, group decision regarding goals and standards is a powerful driving force:

"That the problem of individual morale is to a large extent a social psychological problem of group goals and group standards is thus clear, even in those fields where the person seems to follow individual rather than group goals (Lewin, 1942, 1997, p87)."

"Such a shift would involve...a shift from imposed goals to goals which the group has set for itself...

Experiments in industry under controlled conditions show a substantial permanent increase of production created in a short time by certain methods of 'team decision,' an increase in production that was not accomplished by many months of the usual factory pressure (Lewin, 1944, 1999, p287)."

"For high morale, the objective to be reached will represent a great step forward from the present state of affairs...Morale demands both a goal sufficiently above the present state of affairs, and an effort to reach the distant goal through actions planned with sufficient realism to promise an actual step forward (Lewin, 1942, 1997, p90)."

6. Change as Three Steps

Lewin's approach to planned change is complex yet practical. The unfreeze, move, freeze model, referred to by many (but notably *not* by Lewin) as *Change as Three Steps* (CATS), intentionally simplifies the phenomenon it is describing, as any good theory will. CATS is woven throughout his thinking and writing, not just with those exact words but with field theory concepts such as homeostasis. Lewin's action research is full of references to unfreezing the current homeostasis (by preferably weakening restraining forces), moving the field (again by changing the configuration of forces that make up the field), and freezing in place a new configuration of forces. To only focus on CATS as some have done, to critique it as too simple, and to miss how it is woven into his universal model of social science and planned change is a mistake.

7. Field Theory

Field theory—a form of systems thinking borrowed from the physical sciences—emerged as one of Lewin's most consistently applied models:

"The basic statements of a field theory are that (a) behavior has to be derived from a totality of coexisting facts, (b) these coexisting facts have the character of a 'dynamic field' in so far as the state of any part of this field depends on every other part of the field (Lewin, 1940, 1997, p187)."

"The constellation of the social field as a whole has to be studied and so reorganized that social events flow differently (Lewin, 1947, 1997, p327)."

"The Field Approach: Culture and Group Life as Quasi-Stationary Processes—Food habits of a group, as well as such phenomena as the speed of production in a factory, are the result of a multitude of forces. Some forces support each other, some oppose each other. Some are driving forces, others restraining forces. Like the velocity of a river, the actual conduct of a group depends upon the level (for instance, the speed of production) at which these conflicting forces reach a state of equilibrium (Lewin, 1943, 1997, p290)."

Lewin's application of field theory to industrial production and morale consistently yielded significant and lasting change:

"Production in a Factory–The output of a factory as a whole or of a work-team frequently shows a relatively constant level of output through an extended period of time. It can be viewed as a quasi-stationary equilibrium. An analysis of the relevant forces is of prime importance for understanding and planning changes (Lewin, 1947, 1997, p319)."

Instead of simply applying pressure/forcing a change, Lewin's research supports identifying and addressing restraining forces as a foundation for successful planned change: "...In the first case, the process...would be accomplished by a state of relatively high tension, in the second case, by a state of relatively low tension. Since increase of tension above a certain degree is likely to be paralleled by higher aggressiveness, higher emotionality, and lower constructiveness, it is clear that as a rule, the second method will be preferable to the high pressure method (Lewin, 1948, 1999, p280)."

Lewin developed methods that reliably decreased the restraining forces, achieved the desired results, were sustainable, and could be replicated by others. His methods not only provide a reliable method for planned change, but also lie at, or at least mirror, the roots of all forms of process improvement: "Rational social management, therefore, proceeds in a spiral of steps each of which is composed of a circle of planning, action, and fact-finding about the result of the action (Lewin, 1946, 1997, p146)."

Never did Lewin claim that planned change didn't run into unplanned challenges. On the contrary, he was clear that it is predictable that *unpredictable challenges will emerge* which must be addressed through a combination of sound methods and will power: "To my mind the differences between success and defeat in such undertakings depends mainly upon the willingness and the guts to pull through such periods (Morrow, 1969, p176)."

He was also clear that while unfreeze and freeze were useful concepts, that nothing is really *frozen*. Systems exist before and after the change in a *quasi-stationary* homeostasis: "Change and constancy are relative concepts; group life is never without change, merely differences in the amount and type of change exist (Lewin, 1947, 1997, p308)."

8. Social Construction of Reality

Lewin's leveraging of group dynamics opens a doorway for influencing individuals at the level of values and beliefs. "Social

Construction of Reality...what exists as reality for the individual is, to a high degree, determined by what is socially accepted as reality... Reality therefore is not an absolute. It differs with the group to which the individual belongs...the general acceptance of a fact or a belief might be the very cause preventing this belief or fact from ever being questioned (Lewin, 1945, 1997, p49)."

Lewin demonstrates in the following example (where the presenting problem was a conflict) that to shift the social construction of reality the social scientist must be mindful not to alienate the people involved (a more detailed exploration of this industrial intervention is in Chapter 11):

"The procedure of the psychologist is based on the hypothesis that the permanent conflict is at least partly the result of some faulty organization of production...

To gain their wholehearted co-operation later on it seems best to start the detailed fact-finding here, and it is also necessary to have the first suggestions for the new rules of production worked out by this group.

...if those operators who usually did not make trouble were to initiate a solution, the trouble-makers would probably resist, feeling that they had been first left out and later pushed into something.

...the preliminary interviews have set the stage for this perception (Lewin, 1944, 1997, p97)."

That Lewin did not try to address this conflict by taking on the parental role of enforcing "good behavior" is a subtle yet critical element of planned change. He targeted the technical/production more overtly than the social elements of the system, a focus the group could join with dignity: "The realistic demands of production have to be satisfied in a way which conforms with the nature of group dynamics. To bring about a permanent solution it does not suffice to create amicable relations (Lewin, 1944, 1997, p102)."

Similarly, Lewin viewed passive behavior as a likely restraining force, and active behavior as a driver. Even when training, Lewin applied methods of active participation: "Lecturing is a procedure by which the audience is chiefly passive. The discussion, if conducted correctly, is likely to lead to a much higher degree of involvement (Lewin, 1948, 1999, p271)."

For Lewin the social scientist had to join the system, rather than keep it at arm's length, and certainly must not hold themselves separate from or as better than the people they are assisting: "...in spite of whatever status differences there might be between them, the teacher and the student have to feel as members of one group in matters involving their sense of values.

The chances for re-education seem to increase whenever a strong we-feeling is created (Lewin, 1945, 1997, p55)."

That includes allowing people to speak freely and to think for themselves: "Yet a feeling of complete freedom and a heightened group identification are frequently more important at a particular stage of re-education than learning not to break specific rules (Lewin, 1945, 1997, p55)."

That freedom begins from the first contact, and allows the social scientist to build trust while they begin to influence the social construction of reality: "This attempt to change perception by an 'action interview' (as distinguished from a mere 'fact-finding interview') is one of the basic elements of treatment. By reorienting...perception from the field of personal emotional relationship to the same field of 'objective' facts, the life-spaces which guide the action of these persons have become more similar although the persons themselves are not yet aware of this similarity (Lewin, 1944, 1997 p97)."

9. Everlasting Change for the Betterment of Humanity

Finally, Lewin and his methods were highly experimental, emergent, and agile: "That's what science is all about. Science means progress, and progress means change. True science doesn't admit to stagnation. Everlasting change—that's the essence of science (Marrow, 1969, p23)."

The end goal was planned change for the betterment of humanity: "I am persuaded that scientific sociology and social psychology based on an intimate combination of experiments and empirical theory can do as much, or more, for human betterment as the natural sciences have done (Lewin, 1939, 1997, p67)."

Now we turn to a brief biography of Lewin, which helps introduce you to his methods and theories. True to his formula that behavior is a function of the person *and* the environment, Lewin's social science embodies his personality mixed with lessons learned from the dramatic social and historical context in which he lived.

Section II

A Brief Biography

THE PRACTICAL THEORIST

The Life and Work of
Kurt Lewin

Alfred J. Marrow

Cover of my well-worn copy of
the Lewin biography by Alfred J. Marrow

Chapter 2
The German Years

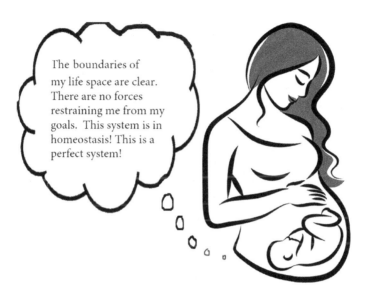

Figure 2.1
Crosby, 2019

Early in life (perhaps not as early as in the drawing, above) Lewin was already thinking about what he called the individual's "life space," and how it was influenced by the groupings (such as family and ethnicity), and the culture one was born into. Lewin was born in Mogilno, in the Prussian province of Posen, (now part of Poland, then part of pre-WWI Germany). As a young Jewish male he quickly learned what social and physical "locomotion" was allowed, and what was verboten—such as becoming a tenured professor at the University of Berlin (verboten!).

By the time he marched off to serve in the Kaiser's army during WWI, Lewin was already theorizing about the nature of being human. He lived his credo that, **"There is nothing so**

practical as a good theory (my bolding) (Lewin, 1943, 1999, p336)." He had earned his doctorate in psychology and was already a pioneer in applying scientific research methods to understanding social phenomena. He was convinced that the explanations of human behavior at the time were inadequate, and that only by combining disciplines such as anthropology, psychology, sociology and in a typically Lewinian creative gesture, topography (the science of map making), could we arrive at a more accurate understanding of ourselves. As Lewin put it, "**I am persuaded that scientific sociology and social psychology based on an intimate combination of experiments and empirical theory can do as much, or more, for human betterment as the natural sciences have done** (my bolding) (Lewin, 1939, 1997, p67)."

Lewin carried this concoction of ideas to the front, where he noted that the way a soldier perceives the environment they are in is a radical departure from how they would perceive the same landscape during peacetime (see Figure 2.2, below). In other words, how we think is influenced by our life circumstances, dramatically so during war, but still true during more "normal" circumstances.

Figure 2.2
Crosby 2020

Lewin rose to the rank of lieutenant. Because he was Jewish, he could rise no higher in the Kaiser's army. In wartime as in peacetime his prospects were limited by prejudice operationalized into law, i.e., *institutional racism*. Lewin was acutely aware of the experience of being a minority with restrictions, as he put it, on "the space of free movement" or "locomotion" not only physical but "social and mental." He began to understand such restrictions in terms of the psychology of motivation combined with the visual tool of topography and the physics concept of counter forces (both driving and restraining) creating a homeostatic field. The following figure (2.3) is an example of Lewin's use of topography to create a visual of "life space." It is a representation of the "space of free movement" of a Jewish male in post WWI Germany, where prejudice was literally legalized.

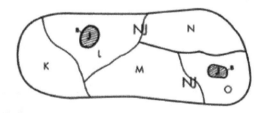

J, Jewish group; *NJ*, non-Jewish group; *B*, barrier between Jewish and non-Jewish groups; *K.L.M.N.O...* may represent geographical areas or occupational fields. As we cannot make use of colors here, we may indicate the degree of similarity between groups by representing the non-Jewish groups as empty regions, the Jewish groups in the Ghetto period as regions with narrow hatching, and the emancipated Jewish groups   as regions with wide hatching.

Figure 2.3
Lewin, 1935, 1997, p110

The following diagram (Figure 2.4) adds force field vectors and Lewin's explanation is full of mathematical representations. Fortunately, as my own career and the career of my father attests, one need not fully understand Lewin's application of physics to social science in order to effectively use his methods. Lewin himself when training people to solve social and organizational problems did not attempt to train them in the math of his topographical psychology. My father took Lewin's force field analysis and came up with his own absolutely non-mathematical visual which you will see in Chapter 13.

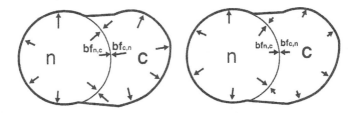

Figure 2.4
Boundary forces and resultant boundary forces (Lewin, 1997, p397)

Meanwhile, as you surely know (amazingly, partially because of the on-going authoritarian battle against reason which Lewin warns us about in Chapter 6, far too many people don't), social conditions for the Jewish minority in Germany would only get worse. Hitler, an elected official, would become an authoritarian dictator.

No wonder, as psychologist Gordon Allport once wrote about Lewin and his contemporary peer, American educator John Dewey, "both recognized that each generation must learn democracy anew (Marrow, 1969, p234)." Democracy requires both skilled leadership and "voluntary and responsible participation," as Lewin's own research will reveal later in this text.

Following the war Lewin returned to his teaching position at the world-renowned Psychological Institute at the University of Berlin, where he broke down boundaries between disciplines, and between students and faculty. His unorthodox approach to teaching included long discussions in coffee shops with his students, in which he demonstrated equal regard for their opinions regardless of ethnicity or gender. In a tribute written soon after Lewin's death (he died in 1947 at the young age of 56), friend and colleague Rensis Likert summed up Lewin this way, "No statement about Lewin and his work would be adequate which failed to mention his qualities as a person. There have been few teachers who have been as devoted and loyal to their students. There are few men who are as sincere and generous in their dealings with their fellow men. There are so few genuinely kind persons that it is a real loss to all of us not to have Lewin among us (Likert, 1947, p3)."

His was a radical approach at the time, especially at the stodgy University of Berlin, where most professors would not allow any discourse between students and faculty. At a time when teaching was authoritarian and questions were verboten, in Lewin's classroom questions and dialogue were encouraged. Another colleague, Ken Benne, describes Lewin's passion for dialog this way, "He was prepared to learn along with anyone —he seemed to be unusually free of status consciousness. He listened and questioned avidly. From time to time he would raise a finger of his right hand and say, 'Aha! Could it be this way?' And he would then propose a new conceptualization of the problem that more often than not opened up a new way of seeing it and new avenues toward a solution (Benne, 1976, p28)."

A great source on Lewin is Alfred Marrow's *The Practical Theorist* (pictured at the beginning of section one). Here is some choice material from Marrow to give you a better feel for Lewin and for that period in his life:

One student, Maria Ovsiankina, reflected on her first class with Lewin, in 1924. "He was discussing some research on memory... It was a seminar and there were only about fifteen of us in the room. What impressed me most was that Lewin was concerned not just with concepts but with behavior. He was young and tried to encourage classroom participation... (Marrow, 1969, p21)." Another student, Tamara Dembo adds, "He was already talking in terms of forces, goal-directed behavior, and the life situation, which later became the life space. For Lewin, Psychology was his whole life. We also thought about it all the time, not as a profession but as our whole way of life too—and a way of life that required precise answers, for Lewin would never accept an answer that was just good enough. So he always had time to talk about one's work, and our answers were refined through the discussion (Marrow, 1969, p21)."

The dialogue during class and after was electrifying. As student Norman Maier put it, "The interaction between Lewin and this group of students was so free, and the disagreement so intense, that I remember them as the most stimulating experiences I have ever had. Historical approaches to psychological problems were swept aside. It seemed as if all questions were being attacked from scratch...These were creative discussions during which ideas and theories were generated, explored, and controverted. I'm sure that Lewin owes much to his students in working through the theories that he himself finally reached (Marrow, 1969, p24)."

The teaching style was as spontaneous as the coffee house discussions. Lewin drew formulas and graphics on his blackboard, and invented as he taught. As student Vera Mahler put it, "Time after time he would interrupt his lecture about some aspect of child psychology, for example, and begin to draw funny little 'eggs' on the blackboard. These he called the 'total psychological field' or 'life space' of the child's world. These little ovals would in turn contain smaller circles representing the child himself, and containing plus and minus signs; arrows would appear to indicate the direction of the various field forces; thick lines represented the barriers. Quickly we were in the midst of a conflict in the child's life, or a situation representing reward and punishment. All this was graphic, all was made clear, in Lewin's little drawings on the blackboard (Marrow, 1969, p22)." The following such graphic (Figure 2.5) is from Lewin, 1946, 1997, p359:

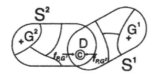

State of indecision. S^1 and S^2 are the two possibilities with their goals G^1 and G^2. D is a region of making a decision.

Figure 2.5
State of indecision

Mahler continues, "We would sit in our seats in the classroom completely absorbed, as Lewin began to develop his train of thought. I shouldn't say he lectured—he really didn't in a conventional, well-organized manner. He was often creating as he was speaking. Frequently he paused in mid-sentence and seemed to forget his audience. Thinking aloud, he vented the new ideas pouring quickly into his mind (Marrow, 1969, p23)."

At times, reports Mahler, this made it difficult for his students. She says she once complained to him, "How can we find our way when you keep coming up with new ideas that sometimes contradict the old ones we haven't yet thoroughly understood?" According to Mahler, Lewin smiled and replied,

"That's what science is all about. Science means progress, and progress means change. True science doesn't admit to stagnation. Everlasting change–that's the essence of science (my bolding) (Marrow, 1969, p23).**"**

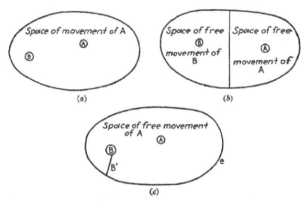

Space of free movement, (*a*) Spaces of movement of *A* and *B* are not separated;(*b*) they are
separated;(*c*)

Figure 2.6
Space of free movement (Lewin, 1936, p75)

Figure 2.6 (above) is another example of Lewin's application of topology to social sience. Lewin kept that experimental spirit throughout his life, with some of his most creative breakthroughs coming in his final days. In that spirit of experiment, Lewin shattered boundaries between disciplines. He was a pioneer in asserting that the research methods used by the physical sciences, including math formulas, could also be applied to understanding social and psychological phenomena. "I am persuaded that it is possible to undertake experiments in sociology which have as much right to be called scientific experiments as those in physics and chemistry (Lewin, 1939, 1997, p59)." Throughout the 1920s Lewin and his students proved his hypothesis by conducting ground-breaking study after study: of emotion, of "levels of aspiration" (the degree of difficulty of the goal), of tension (in relationship to goals), all in the context of field theory (the interplay of forces that maintain or break homeostasis) and the interplay between the individual and the environment. The subjects of their research were often children, and many of the experiments were captured on film. Figure 2.7, below, is another example of topology being applied to psychology.

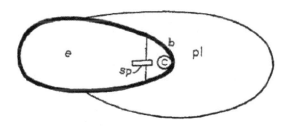

Topology of an eating situation: a child is prohibited from leaving for play. *c*, child; *b*, barrier (mother's interference); *e*, region of eating; *sp*, spoon; *pl*, region of play.

Figure 2.7
Topology of an eating situation (Lewin, 1936, p81)

Radical at the time, and still poorly understood by many, Lewin came up with his famous systems thinking formula during his Institute of Psychology years:

$$B = f\ (P,E)$$

Behavior is a function of the person and the environment. Then and now, most people, when push comes to shove, believe that behavior is mostly a reflection of individual personality. When there are performance problems in organizations, the focus is on individuals. People are shuffled around, hired and fired in hopes of "putting the right people on the bus." Lewin understood that the social bus (the primary groups in a person's life, the organization, the society) has a huge influence on beliefs and behavior. Change the system, and you have the most reliable chance of changing the individual. His planned change methods fully incorporate this type of systems thinking, as we shall see.

By the early 1930s the system he was in, Germany during the rise of Nazism, was unbearable (Figure 2.8, below). Lewin began looking for a way out. The way out proved to be the United States. He was invited as a visiting professor at Stanford in 1932.

In 1933, as a professor, Lewin managed to breach a barrier that many of his family and friends could not.

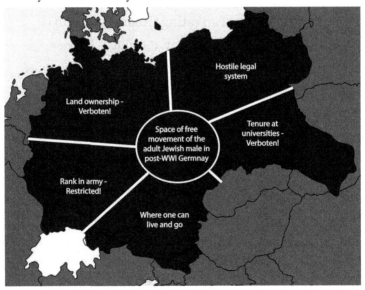

Figure 2.8
Space of free movement for a Jewish male in pre and post WWI Germany, Crosby, 2020

In Germany it was almost impossible for Jewish citizens to liquefy assets and raise the funds needed for immigration; in the United States it was almost impossible for Jewish immigrants to be granted admittance, despite their obvious need. Anti-Semitism ran deep in the United States. In 1922, for example, Harvard President Abbott Lawrence Lowell publicly proposed a quota system to limit the number of Jewish students (Marrow, 1969, p101). The trustee's rejected his proposal, but similar overtly racist sentiments were present in much of America's culture. In 1931, when Lewin was applying for an academic post in the United States, eminent psychologist E.G. Boring of Harvard wrote to Stanford professor L. Terman that, "In the first place Lewin is a Jew... also the wife is a Jew and their child, who has figured in some of the movies of Lewin's child psychology, is a 'perfect little yid' (Winston, 1996)."

Despite these barriers, Lewin and his wife and daughter made it to the U.S. His extended family did not. Lewin frantically did everything he could, for family and for others, even trying in 1941 to get a Cuban entry visa for his mother. As he put it in a letter to Alfred Marrow, "We have sent something like $2600 to Cuba, and have the official receipts here. We have a photostatic copy of the wire sent to Germany by the Cuban government... but the Cuban consulate in Germany says it has not received it... we finally got the Cuban government to send a second wire." Despite his relentless efforts, he got no help from the US State Department. Sometime in 1943 his mother was shipped from Holland to Poland. (Marrow, 1969, p140). By 1944 his mother had died in a Nazi gas chamber (Benne, 1976, p28).

Chapter 3
The USA Years

Despite the anti-Semitism of his new country, Lewin embraced the USA whole-heartedly (and no doubt with great relief despite separating from his extended family) and passionately set out to strengthen democracy here and abroad in all of his activities. He also dove into our customs with glee, stating to Alfred Marrow at the 1939 New York World's Fair, "Let's have a couple of hot dogs. That's what we Americans eat on Sunday evenings in the summer (Marrow, 1969, p171)."

Here are some key dates:

1929: Lecturer at Yale International Congress of Psychology where he presents his film of his 18-month-old niece Hannah attempting to sit on a rock. Despite a language barrier, the film allowed Lewin to convey his concepts to the stodgy audience, including that of forces in a field. As Marrow put it, "Little Hannah had passed the stone many times before without wanting to sit on it. When she finally did want to... it was because she was tired (Marrow, 1969, p50)." The object (the stone) held no meaning to her until her life space was altered by fatigue. It's also an excellent example of how, unlike his predecessors and contemporaries, Lewin considered all variables, including physiological states, as relevant to the psychology and behavior of the individual.

1932: Lewin is a guest lecturer at Stanford (despite Boring's racist remarks) and makes the contacts that lead to securing a faculty position in the United States, a pre-requisite to his ability to immigrate.

1933: Guest lecturer at the University of Cambridge (during his journey to the United States) where he met Eric Trist, also guest lecturer at Harvard for the entire spring semesters in 1938 & 1939, the Menninger Clinic in Topeka, Kansas, the University of California at Berkeley for the summer session of 1939, amongst other constant speaking and lecturing invitations (Marrow, 1969, p138).

As a psychology student, Trist, who went on to found London's Tavistock Institute, had stumbled upon one of Lewin's articles in the Cambridge library. As he tells it, "It was a revelation. When I returned to the department, Professor Bartlett asked me, 'What happened to you?' My eyes were evidently sparkling. I told him about this extraordinary paper. My interest in and debt to Lewin began at that moment." A year later, when Lewin visited Professor Bartlett on his way to America, Eric Trist was one of those whom Bartlett invited to tea (Marrow, 1969, p69).

1933-1936: Lewin becomes a refugee scholar with temporary (two year) appointment at Cornell University's School of Home Economics in Ithaca, NY, by a grant from the Emergency Committee on Displaced Scholars (Marrow, 1969, p74). Meets Rensis Likert for the first time en route to Cornell.

1935: Publication of his first book, *A Dynamic Theory of Personality*.

1936: Publication of *Some Social-Psychological Differences Between the United States and Germany*.

The Cover of Lewin's second book

1936: Publication of his second book (actually written in Germany but never published there), *Principles of Topological Psychology*.

1933 until the mid 1940s: Lewin attempts to found a Psychological Institute at the Hebrew University in Jerusalem. Alfred Marrow credits this effort as the foundation for Lewin's conceptualization of "Action Research (Marrow, 1969, p82)."

1936-1944: Appointed for initial three-year position at the University of Iowa Child Welfare Research Station (Marrow, 1969, p84).

1939-1946: At CEO Alfred Marrow's invitation, begins Action Research at Harwood Manufacturing's rural Virginia plant.

Marrow's father and grandfather had founded Harwood together in 1899 (Burns, 2019, p4). Marrow, who also had a doctorate degree, "...met Lewin in 1934 when he consulted Lewin about his PhD topic (Burns, 2019, p5)." He and Lewin became friends and formed a remarkable partnership. Marrow, in partnership with Lewinian experts such as John French and Ron Lippitt, continued using, refining, and documenting Lewin's organization development methods for decades, and had a significant impact on the development of the profession (Burns, 2019, p7). He was the kind of executive sponsor that OD professionals dream of and, thankfully, occasionally find.

1937-1939 (Approximate dates): Boy's groups studies with Lippitt and White at the University of Iowa, including publication of *Experiments on Autocratic and Democratic Atmospheres*.

1942-1944: Colleague Margaret Mead solicits Lewin's participation in the U.S. Dept. of Agriculture Committee on Food Habits studies. Mead and Lewin were yet another amazing collaboration.

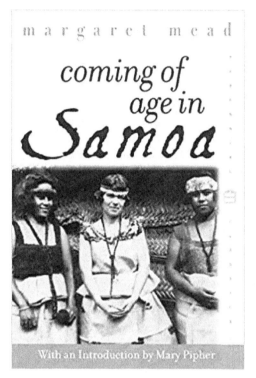

margaret mead

coming of age in

Samoa

With an Introduction by Mary Pipher

Lewin's groundbreaking colleague, Margaret Mead

1939: The Nazis invade Poland. Lewin predicts that the spread of the Nazis in Europe will only get worse.

1939: Publication of *Experiments in Social Space* (Lewin, 1939, 1997, p59-67). Lewin's first use of the term "group dynamics" (Marrow, 1969, p168).

1942: Publication of *Time Perspective and Morale*.

1943: Publication of *Cultural Reconstruction* and *The Special Case of Germany*.

1944: Lewin simultaneously founds the Research Center for Group Dynamics at M.I.T. and the Commission on Community Interrelations (C.C.I.) for the American Jewish Congress (Marrow, 1969, p173).

According to Lewin, "The Center would educate research workers in theoretical and applied fields of group life and assist in training practitioners. The main task of the Center would be the development of scientific methods of studying and changing group life and the development of concepts and theories of group dynamics (Marrow, 1969, p172)."

Marrow (1969, p184) documents that the Research Center for Group Dynamics identified six program areas:

1. Group productivity
2. Communication and the spread of influence
3. Social perception
4. Intergroup relations
5. Group membership and individual adjustment
6. The training of leaders and the improvement of group functioning

Along with an all-star staff including Ronald Lippitt (who mentored my father for decades), the location of the Center gave Lewin easy access to collaborate with the likes of Douglas McGregor at the Department of Economics and Social Science at M.I.T. and Gordon Allport at Harvard. The far-flung circles influencing and to a greater degree influenced by Lewin continued to grow (Marrow, 1969, p182).

Always working at an amazing pace (perhaps too fast for his health), Lewin published many articles towards the end of his life. I'm only listing the highlights from my perspective here:

My primary source

1944: Publication of *The Solution of a Chronic Conflict in Industry*.

1944: Publication of *The Dynamics of Group Action*.

1945: Publication of *Conduct, Knowledge, and Acceptance of New Values*.

1946: Publication of *Action Research and Minority Problems*.

1947: Publication of *Frontiers in Group Dynamics*.

1947: February 11th, Lewin dies of a heart attack.

Section III
Methods and Theories

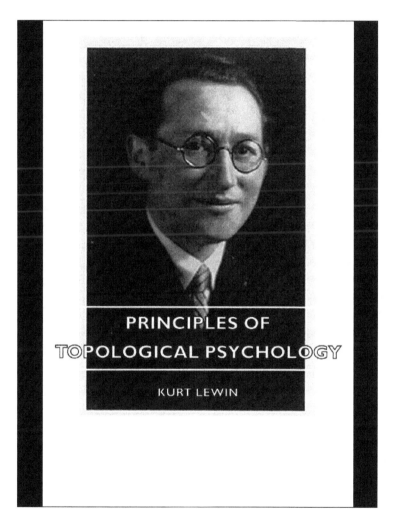

Cover for Lewin's second book, version 2

Chapter 4
A Universal Theory of Social Science

Physicists have long sought a universal theory that explains all phenomena, whether relatively small or large. Lewin set the bar no lower for the social sciences. He was determined to establish a universal theory of social science that could be used to understand and effect change at the individual, group, and societal level. While acknowledging that small individual behaviors could not be predicted, such as which pair of pants I might chose tomorrow morning, Lewin believed that the majority of beliefs and behaviors could be reliably understood, influenced, and even predicted in the context of the system they are in. As Lewin put it, "One of the most striking features of this development (the transition from Aristotelian to Galilean concepts) is that the opposition between universal concept and individual event is overcome. Law and single occurrence enter into intimate relationship... Thereby the representation of single cases gains new scientific meaning. It has a direct bearing on the determination of general laws (Lewin, 1936, p21)."

I believe I can and will demonstrate that Lewin achieved his goal of establishing social science theory and methods that can be applied universally to understanding and influencing human behavior. To the extent that he was thwarted in any portion of his quest, it would be in his vision of complementing his theories with a system for representing social phenomena in mathematical and topographical terms. That remains an unfinished task, perhaps unachievable, but that does not detract from the quality of his theories and methods.

His success in establishing a theory that covers both "universal concept and individual event" is a blessing both to my professional career and to humanity. Unfortunately, it also makes the task of organizing his writing into discreet topics more difficult and somewhat arbitrary. For example, some of Lewin's best planned change writing came in his 1943 essays on the impending cultural reconstruction of Germany. Is it political analysis? Is it about group dynamics? Social change? Organization development (OD)? The answer is all of the above, because as he intended, Lewin's core theoretical thinking applied to everything related to human behavior, both large and small, general and singular.

I realize that I lived much of my life without reading some of his best writing. This was in part because I never thought to look under some of his article headings. What for example, one might think at first glance, has *The Special Case of Germany* got to do with my work as an OD practitioner? Much to my pleasant surprise, it turns out, when you start to take in the sub-headings such as 1) *General Aspects of Culture Change*, and 2) *Techniques of Changing Culture*, this and most of his writing is relevant to everything OD. This realization was an important part of my motivation to weave his words together in this text.

Along with his belief that a universal theoretical approach could be devised, Lewin believed that advancement in the social sciences is critical to averting the destructive power of technology and securing a better future for humanity.

As he put it in the beginning of one of his last essays, *Frontiers in Group Dynamics* (Lewin, 1947, 1997, p301):

One of the by-products of the second World War of which society is hardly aware is the new stage of development which the social sciences have reached. This development indeed may prove to be as revolutionary as the atom bomb. Applying cultural anthropology to modern rather than "primitive" cultures, experimentation with groups inside and outside the laboratory, the measurement of socio-psychological aspects of large social bodies, the combination of economic, cultural, and psychological fact-finding—all of these developments started before the war. But, by providing unprecedented facilities and by demanding realistic and workable solutions to scientific problems, the war has accelerated greatly the change of social sciences to a new developmental level.

The scientific aspects of this development center around three objectives:

1. Integrating social sciences.
2. Moving from the description of social bodies to dynamic problems of changing group life.
3. Developing new instruments and techniques of social research.

Theoretical progress has hardly kept pace with the development of techniques. It is, however, as true for the social as for the physical and biological sciences that without adequate conceptual development, science cannot proceed beyond a certain stage... The theoretical development will have to proceed rather rapidly if social science is to reach that level of practical usefulness which society needs for winning the race against the destructive capacities set free by man's use of the natural sciences (as illustrated in Figure 4.1).

Figure 4.1
Mushroom cloud

With a sense of urgency, Lewin brought us a long long way quickly. It may be easy to take systems thinking for granted these days. On the other hand, if you blame most problems on individual abilities, personalities, or groups, you are still stuck in pre-systemic thinking. As Rensis Likert explains, Lewin opened the door to changing that:

"One of the clearest and simplest formulations of Kurt Lewin was his distinction between the scientific concepts of Aristotle and Galileo. In dynamics Aristotle emphasized the 'nature' of the object: he held that a stone fell to the ground because it was 'earth' and had therefore to go towards the earth. Galileo, on the other hand, made physicists pay more attention to the object's relation to its environment. According to Aristotelian thought the environment played a part by 'disturbing' the processes which followed from the nature of the object concerned; but in Galileian thought it is the concrete whole, which comprises the object and the situation, that determines the dynamics of the event defined: that is to say, an object is always in and part of its environment - an obvious notion, but one with far-reaching implications if taken literally and always applied (Likert, 1947, p3)."

Figure 4.2
Galileo Galilei

This is no small shift in perspective. As Lewin puts it, "...the transition from Aristotelian to Galilean concepts demands that we no longer seek the 'cause' of events in the nature of a single object, but in the relationship between an object and its surroundings. It is not thought then that the environment of the individual serves merely to facilitate or inhibit tendencies which are established once for all in the nature of the person. One can hope to understand the forces that govern behavior only if one includes in the representation the whole psychological situation (Lewin, 1936, p26)."

Systems Thinking: The Object and Its Surroundings

Or to put it another way, in systems thinking what is happening in the "object" is a window into "its surroundings" and vice versa. The part reflects the whole, influences the whole, and is influenced by the whole. To change the object (an individual, a group, a location) one must understand, address, and change enough of the system to influence the object and sustain the change. Or, as family systems thinker Edwin Friedman might put it, the object of focus is the symptom bearer or "identified patient" in which the system's "stress or pathology has surfaced" and if you treat it in isolation "fundamental change is not likely (Friedman, 1985, p19)."

Lewin constantly bridged the gap between theories and disciplines, and my orientation is to do the same. A prime example is how clearly Lewin's concepts blend with Friedman and his mentor Murray Bowen's family systems theory. The synergy between Bowen's theories and Lewin's is striking. Both took a highly inter-disciplinary approach, both applied biological concepts such as differentiation, physics concepts such as field theory, psychological concepts such as the effect of tension on individuals and groups, and homeostasis (from physics and biology). Bowen (and his protégé Friedman) are the next biggest influences after Lewin on my version of OD (with John Wallen, Daniel Goleman, and Daryl Conner close behind).

I suspect Bowen (1913-1990) was influenced by Lewin, but I have found no evidence yet in the form of citations in Bowen or Friedman's materials. However, besides the parallels in their theoretical material, Bowen was at the Menninger Foundation in Topeka, Kansas, from 1946 to 1954, where Lewin had been a guest lecturer, and he formulated his major theories during the 1950s when Lewin's influence in psychology circles was strong. The similarities make it so that Bowen and Friedman, as well as others, can easily be applied to and enrich Lewinian theory. I trust Lewin would agree, especially perhaps about the usefulness of *The Interpersonal Gap* by John Wallen (Appendix A), which wasn't formulated until years after Lewin's death. I will occasionally point out such theoretical synergies throughout this text.

Field Theory: The Life Space

In Lewin's mind, one could best operationalize systems thinking and better understand the relationship between the object and its surroundings by thinking in terms of fields. The current moment, or "life space" of the individual, includes the field of the real and imagined past as it is relevant in the moment, as well as the field of goals and aspirations towards the future. "According to field theory, behavior depends neither on the past nor on the future but on the present field. (This present field has a certain time-depth. It includes the 'psychological past,' 'psychological present,' and 'psychological future' which constitute one of the dimensions of the life space existing at a given time.) (Lewin, 1945, 1997, p189)."

It also includes the relevant fields of the individual's primary groupings, which could be as small as a one on one relationship, a family, a work group, and as large as an ethnic group, one's gender, a nation, or even the human race. Behavior in the moment is related to and a reflection of these social fields, although not everything is relevant at any given time, nor can all behaviors be predicted. As Lewin put it, "Although the whole life situation always has some influence on the behavior, the extent to which one must take it explicitly into account... is very different in different cases. A person who is trying to decide whether or not to get married, whether or not to go into a certain business, whether or not to begin a lawsuit against an influential opponent, will in general act in accord with his whole life situation.

Only happy-go-lucky, superficial, or childish persons act out of a narrow momentary situation in important questions of life. On the other hand whether a man who is taking a walk goes along the right or the left side of the road will be decided by a much less inclusive momentary situation. It is easy to observe how the structured part of the life space becomes wider or narrower under the influence of a new event (Lewin, 1936, p43)."

The object and its surroundings, the general law and the specific instance, the past and future; all important elements of Lewin's universal social science. All elements of the life space of individuals and groups at any given point in time. "... the psychological field which exists at a given time contains also the views of that individual about his future and past. The individual sees not only his present situation; he has certain expectations, wishes, fears, daydreams for his future. His views about his own past and that of the rest of the physical and social world are often incorrect but nevertheless constitute, in his life space, the 'reality-level' of the past. In addition, a wish-level in regard to the past can frequently be observed. The discrepancy between the structure of this wish—or irreality—level of the psychological past and the reality—level plays an important role in the phenomenon of guilt. The structure of the psychological future is closely related, for instance, to hope and planning (Lewin, 1943, 1997, p207)."

Socially Constructed Reality

The subjective and socially constructed nature of personal reality (or irreality) is also a vital concept in Lewin's methods. Boldly reaching across disciplines, anthropology provided much of the research that grounded Lewin's belief that culture and values were social constructs and as such could be altered and were best altered through social (group) process. *We are products of the cultural field that we are born into.* "Cultural anthropology has emphasized recently that any constancy of culture is based on the fact that children are growing into that culture. They are indoctrinated and habituated in childhood in a way that keeps their habits strong enough for the rest of their lives (Lewin, 1943, 1997, p290)." As he put it later in *Conduct, Knowledge, and Acceptance of New Values*, **"...what exists as reality for the individual is, to a high degree, determined by what is socially accepted as reality.** This holds even in the field of physical fact: to the South Sea Islander the world may be flat; to the European it is round. **Reality therefore is not an absolute. It differs with the group to which the individual belongs...the general acceptance of a fact or a belief might be the very cause preventing this belief or fact from ever being questioned** (my bolding) (Lewin, 1945, 1997, p49)." I believe that Lewin's methods for changing beliefs, which we will explore in detail, still set the standard today.

Intention, Tension, and Aspiration

The tension inherent in future orientation, intention, goal orientation and/or aspiration plays a vital role in Lewinian theory. Overseeing and drawing on the research of his students, as he often did, Lewin put it this way (1940, 1997, p174): "The critical experiments about association and 'the measurement of will power' mentioned above had suggested the theory that the effect of an intention was equivalent to the creation of an inner personal tension. The purpose of Zeigarnik's experiment was to provide a first experimental test of this theory. The theory contains two basic assumptions.

(A1) Assumption 1: The intention to reach a certain goal G (to carry out an action leading to G) corresponds to a tension (t) in a certain system (SG) within the person so that t(SG) >0. This assumption coordinates a dynamic construct (system in tension) with the observable syndrome popularly called 'intention.'

(A2) Assumption 2: The tension t(SG) is released if the goal G is reached."

In Lewin's mind, Assumption 2 is represented by the following formula:

$$t(S^G) = 0 \text{ if } P \subset G$$

Figure 4.3
Assumption 2 (Lewin, 1940, 1997, p175)

Tension in the field of the life space is subsequently the foundation for Lewin's understanding of conflict, as he explains in *The Background of Conflict in Marriage* (Lewin 1940, 1997, p71):

The General Conditions of Conflict

Experimental studies on individuals and groups show that one of the most important factors in the frequency of conflict and in the building up of an emotional outbreak is the general level of tension at which the person or group lives (see Figure 4.4, facing page). Whether or not a particular event will lead to a conflict depends largely on the tension level or on the social atmosphere in the group. Among the causes for tension the following may be listed as outstanding:

1. The degree to which the needs of a person are in a state of hunger or satisfaction. A need in the state of hunger means not only that a particular region within the person is under tension but also that the person as a whole is on a higher tension level. This holds particularly for basic needs, such as sex or security.

2. The amount of space of free movement of the person. Too small a space of free movement generally leads to a high state of tension. This has been shown in experiments with anger and with democratic and autocratic group atmosphere. In an autocratic atmosphere the tension is much higher, resulting in apathy or aggression.

3. Outer barrier. Tension or conflict lead frequently to a tendency to leave the unpleasant situation. If this is possible, no high tension will develop. Lack of freedom to leave the situation as a result of either an "outer barrier" or an inner bond greatly favors the development of high tension and conflict.

4. Within the group life conflicts depend upon the degree to which the goals of the members contradict each other, and upon the readiness to consider the other person's point of view.

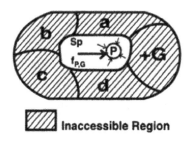

Tension in situation of frustration and narrow space of free movement. P, person; G, goal; Sp, space of free movement; a, b, c, d, inaccessible regions; $f_{P,G}$, force acting on P in the direction of G.

Figure 4.4
Tension in situation of frustration and narrow space of free movement (Lewin, 1940, 1997, p72)

This leads us back in the direction of one of Lewin's most famous theoretical formulas:

What is accomplished in regard to representing psychological relations by means of topological and vector concepts, and what should be the next objectives? If I may express my own feeling about this question, which will be answered properly, of course, only by the future development of psychology, I would stress the following points:

The possibilities of a field theory in the realm of action, emotion, and personality are firmly established. **The basic statements of a field theory are that a) behavior has to be derived from a totality of coexisting facts, and b) these coexisting facts have the character of a "dynamic field" in so far as the state of any part of this field depends on every other part of the field.** The proposition (a) includes the statement that we have to deal in psychology, too, with a manifold, the interrelations of which cannot be represented without the concept of space. In fact all psychological schools implicitly agree with this statement by using concepts like approach or withdrawal, social position, and so forth in their descriptions. It is more and more recognized, although there are still some exceptions, that the spatial relations of psychological data cannot be adequately represented by means of the physical space, but have to be treated, at least for the time being, as a psychological space. It is everywhere accepted that this "life space" includes the person and the psychological environment.

In regard to proposition (b) the situation is similar. Even theories originally based on a coordination of isolated stimuli to isolated reactions have developed in a direction which brings them at least very close to (b). A good example for this is the theory of Hull, which does not correlate a reaction to a single stimulus such as an optical one, but to a "pattern of stimuli" which includes goal and drive stimuli. In principle it is everywhere accepted that **behavior (B) is a function of the person (P) and the environment (E), B=F(P,E)**, and that P and E in this formula are interdependent variables (my bolding) (Lewin, 1940, 1997, p187).

The individual must be understood in relationship to its surroundings. Change the beliefs and behaviors of one's primary groups, and you almost certainly change the individual. Change the individual alone and put it back in the same field, and the change will almost certainly regress. Personally, I think the formula should be skewed towards the power of the social/group influences. I think Lewin's research and methods reflect the same. We all as individuals influence the systems we are in, but if we differentiate too much from the system we will be rejected. The influence of the social field we were born into is powerful and subtle. It is easy to have blind spots to our own version of the socially constructed reality, and to think we are simply seeing things as they are.

With Lewin's help, we will kick these ideas around throughout this text. Keep in mind as we explore these ideas that Lewin was constantly doing the same. He would expect us to clarify theory and continually develop and refine it through real world application. As he famously said,

"**There is nothing as practical as a good theory** (Lewin, 1943, 1999, p336)."

The importance of applied theory is indeed another foundation of his theoretical approach. Here we make the subtle shift from theory to method, supported by *theories about methods*. Indeed, Lewin saw some theories inherently as methods: "Field theory is probably best characterized as a method: namely, a method of analyzing causal relations and of building scientific constructs (Lewin, 1943, 1997, p201)."

Lewin was dogmatic in his belief that theory helps us understand and simplify complex phenomena and situations, so that we can have an organized approach. It also allows us to test and adjust our beliefs in a continuous learning cycle. By applying theory to real-world problems, we both test the theory and take action on the problems simultaneously. Lewin highly valued the blending of research and action, as is evident in yet another of his most famous quotes:

"**No research without action, no action without research** (Marrow, 1969, p193)."

Lewin adhered to this principle and advanced our knowledge considerably. Looking at his statistical assessments, which are sprinkled throughout this section, is both eye opening, and for me at least, a treat. In his 1946 paper, *Action Research and Minority Problems*, Lewin, ever passionate about application of social science to solve real-world problems, explains: "The research needed for social practice can best be characterized as research for social management or social engineering. It is a type of action-research, a comparative research on the conditions and effects of various forms of social action, and research leading to social action. Research that produces nothing but books will not suffice (Lewin, 1946, 1997, p144)."

Lewin and the terms "action research" came to be synonymous, even though as you shall see his own use of the term was relatively fluid.

According to Alfred Marrow, when Lewin founded the Commission on Community Interrelations (C.C.I.) for the American Jewish Congress in 1944, Lewin oversaw the identification by members of the advisory board (which included chairperson Marrow, Gordon Allpart, Rensis Likert, Douglass McGregor, Margaret Mead, and other all-stars of the social sciences) of following four "varieties of action research: 1) diagnostic, 2) participant, 3) empirical, and 4) experimental (Marrow, 1969, p198)."

Marrow explains the four varieties like this:

1. *Diagnostic* was designed to produce a needed plan of action. Here C.C.I. would step into an already existing situation (for example a race riot or anti-semitic vandalism), diagnose the problem, and recommend remedial measures... however, this design of action was often wasted.

2. *Participant* action research assumed that the residents of the affected community who were to help effect a cure must be involved in the research process from the beginning.

3. *Empirical* action research was primarily a matter of record keeping and accumulating experiences.

4. *Experimental* action research called for a controlled study of the relative effectiveness of various techniques in nearly identical social situations.

It's no surprise to me that #1, *diagnostic,* an expert model, proved to be "often wasted." More on that to come. *Participant* action research was the model that Lewin conducted the most, and it led to reliable results for Lewin, my father, and many other OD professionals. I've never set out to do variety 3, but I have done it over time with comparative data, and Lewin clearly did the same. Finally, Lewin was master of *experimental* action research, usually, but not always, combining it with the *participant* model so that there was both immediate results and contribution to the knowledge base of the social sciences.

Turning again to *Action Research and Minority Problems,* we find Lewin elaborating further on those two objectives (Lewin, 1946, 1997, p145):

Two Types of Research Objectives

It is important to understand clearly that social research concerns itself with two rather different types of questions, namely the study of general laws of group life and the diagnosis of a specific situation.

Problems of general laws deal with the relation between possible conditions and possible results. They are expressed in "if so" propositions. The knowledge of laws can serve as guidance for the achievement of certain objectives under certain conditions. To act correctly, it does not suffice, however, if the engineer or the surgeon knows the general laws of physics or physiology. He has to know too the specific character of the situation at hand. This character is determined by a scientific fact-finding called diagnosis. For any field of action both types of scientific research are needed.

Until recently, fact-finding on inter-group relations has been largely dominated by surveys. We have become somewhat critical of these surveys of inter-group relations. Although they are potentially important, they have, as a rule, used rather superficial methods of poll taking and not the deeper searching of the interview type used by Likert which gives us some insight into the motivations behind the sentiments expressed.

The second cause of dissatisfaction is the growing realization that mere diagnosis—and surveys are a type of diagnosis—does not suffice. In inter-group relations as in other fields of social management the diagnosis has to be complemented by experimental comparative studies of the effectiveness of various techniques of change (my bolding).

He goes on in the same paper to use the war effort to further describe action research:

In highly developed fields of social management, such as modern factory management or the execution of a war, this second step is followed by certain fact-findings. For example, in the bombing of Germany a certain factory may have been chosen as the first target after careful consideration of various priorities and of the best means and ways of dealing with this target. The attack is pressed home and immediately a reconnaissance plane follows with the one objective of determining as accurately and objectively as possible the new situation.

This reconnaissance or fact-finding has four functions. First, it should evaluate the action. It shows whether what has been achieved is above or below expectation. Secondly, it gives the planners a chance to learn, that is, to gather new general insight, for instance, regarding the strength and weakness of certain weapons or techniques of action.

Thirdly, this fact-finding should serve as a basis for correctly planning the next step. Finally, it serves as a basis for modifying the "overall plan."

The next step again is composed of a circle of planning, executing, and reconnaissance or fact-finding for the purpose of evaluating the results of the second step, for preparing the rational basis for planning the third step, and for perhaps modifying again the overall plan.

Rational social management, therefore, proceeds in a spiral of steps each of which is composed of a circle of planning, action, and fact-finding about the result of the action (my bolding) (Lewin, 1946, 1997, p146).

You may recognize this spiral of steps. It is the foundation for the application of science to incident investigation, process improvement, lean manufacturing, quality management, etc. While Lewin was not the only innovator to apply scientific methods to understanding and improving processes (Taylor came before Lewin, for example), you are no doubt already using Lewinian methodology or something like it in your life, without realizing the source.

And who should do the fact-finding in this circle of experimentation? The expert? Lewin's research pointed away from the purely *diagnostic* model and pointed to the *participant* model. For change to stick, the people facing the problem must do their own diagnosis and generate and implement their own solutions. **"The laws (of social science) don't do the job of diagnosis which has to be done locally. Neither do laws prescribe the strategy for change** (my bolding) (Lewin, 1946, 1997, p150)."

The following is a partial list (all of which are explored in the pages ahead) of Lewin's extensive body of research, which was always done to both achieve immediate results and to advance social science:

Experiments on Autocratic and Democratic Atmospheres (Lewin, 1938)

Food Habits Study (Marrow, 1969, p129)

Time Perspective and Morale (Harwood Manufacturing) (Lewin, 1942, 1997, p80)

Integrated Housing (Marrow, 1969, p208)

Prejudice in Seaside (Changing Gang Behavior)(Marrow, 1969, p203).

Let us turn now to a deeper exploration of Lewin's methods of planned change.

Chapter 5
Planned Change

I get tired of all the hype I read and hear about the pace of change. On the other hand, when Lewin's student and my father's mentor Ron Lippitt speaks, I listen, and he had this to say back in 1958 (the year before I was born):

"The modern world is, above everything else, a world of rapid change. This is something in which observers in every field of thought and knowledge are agreed. What does it mean? Many things of course but perhaps its primary meaning lies in its effect upon people. It means that people, too, must change, must acquire an unaccustomed facility for change, if they are to live in the modern world...It means that if we are to maintain our health and a creative relationship with the world around us, we must be actively engaged in change efforts directed toward ourselves and toward our material, social, and spiritual environments (Lippitt et al, 1958, p3)."

In his co-authored book, *The Dynamics of Planned Change*, Lippitt offers this simple definition:

"...*planned change* ... a deliberate effort to improve the system... (Lippitt et al, 1958, p10)."

That brings us to one of Lewin's best known and most controversial models. Published with only minor alterations in two different articles *Frontiers in Group Dynamics* (Lewin 1947, 1997, p330) and *Group Decision and Social Change* (Lewin, 1948, 1999, p282), Lewin summarized the process of planned change this way.

Changing as Three Steps: Unfreezing, Moving, and Freezing of Group Standards

A change toward a higher level of group performance is frequently short lived; after a "shot in the arm," group life soon returns to the previous level. This indicates that it does not suffice to define the objective of a planned change in group performance as the reaching of a different level. Permanency of the new level, or permanency for a desired period, should be included in the objective. A successful change includes therefore three aspects: unfreezing (if necessary) the present level L1, moving to the new level L2, and freezing group life on the new level. Since any level is determined by a force field, permanency implies that the new force field is made relatively secure against change.

The "unfreezing" of the present level may involve quite different problems in different cases. Allport has described the "catharsis" which seems to be necessary before prejudices can be removed. To break open the shell of complacency and self-righteousness it is sometimes necessary to bring about deliberately an emotional stir-up.

The same holds for the problem of freezing the new level. Sometimes it is possible to establish an organizational setup which is equivalent to a stable circular causal process.

Critics of Lewin have said this model of *change as three steps* (dubbed CATS by some) is too simple. I counter such criticism at a number of levels, the first being that the same could be said of the simplification of any phenomenon, and that simplification, in the right dose, is very helpful. Unfreezing, moving, and freezing is an intentional simplification, to create a framework for the process of planned change. Lewin was well aware that the actual effort of changing something is complicated and full of setbacks and surprises, many of which emerge along the way. He is often quoted as saying[1],

"If you want to understand something, try to change it."

---

1. I could not locate a source for this quote, even though I could buy a notebook on Amazon with this quote on the cover attributed to Lewin.

Lewin never assumed smooth sailing in any action research or other venture. As he was giving birth to the Commission on Community Interrelations, in a letter to his funding source, Lewin put it this way, "I know that we will have to face an unknown number of obstacles, the most severe of which, I am sure, is hidden from us at present. The sailing for a while may be easier than I expect. But somewhere along the road, maybe in a half-year, maybe in two years, I am sure we will have to face major crisis. I have observed this type of development in many research undertakings, and we will have to be unusually lucky if this time we avoid it. **To my mind the difference between success and defeat in such undertakings depends mainly upon the willingness and the guts to pull through such periods.** It seems to me decisive that one knows that such developments are the rule, that one is not afraid of this period, and that one holds up a team that is able to pull through (my bolding) (Morrow, 1969, p176)."

Diving into the complexity of change, Lewin writes, "To change the level of velocity of a river its bed has to be narrowed down or widened, rectified, cleared from rocks, etc. To decide how best to bring about such an actual change, it does not suffice to consider one property. The total circumstances have to be examined. For changing a social equilibrium, too, one has to consider the total social field: the groups and subgroups involved, their relations, their value systems, etc. **The constellation of the social field as a whole has to be studied and so reorganized that social events flow differently** (my bolding) (Lewin, 1947, 1997, p327)."

With such complexity in mind, Lewin devised methods of planned change that address enough of the "constellation of the social field as a whole" to reliably implement and sustain the desired outcomes.

He was also quite clear that freezing at the new level is not some sort of final or permanent condition. Change is continuous. "**Change and constancy are relative concepts; group life is never without change, merely differences in the amount and type of change exist** (my bolding) (Lewin, 1947, 1997, p308)." On the other hand, his research, validated by the experience of my father, my colleagues, and I, show that through his basic methods a new and resilient homeostasis can reliably be achieved.

In his 1943 essay, *Psychological Ecology* (Lewin, 1943, 1997, p290), Lewin uses his *Food Habits* action research as an example for explaining his theory of planned change, including the application of group dynamics and field theory.

The Field Approach: Culture and Group Life as Quasi-Stationary Processes

This question of planned change or of any "social engineering" is identical with the question: What "conditions" have to be changed to bring about a given result and how can one change these conditions with the means at hand?

One should view the present situation—the status quo—as being maintained by certain conditions or forces. A culture —for instance, the food habits of a given group at a given time —is not a static affair but a live process like a river which moves but still keeps a recognizable form. In other words, we have to deal, in group life as in individual life, with what is known in physics as "quasi-stationary" processes.

Food habits do not occur in empty space. They are part and parcel of the daily rhythm of being awake and asleep; of being alone and in a group; of earning a living and playing; of being a member of a town, a family, a social class, a religious group, a nation; of living in a hot or a cool climate; in a rural area or a city, in a district with good groceries and restaurants or in an area of poor and irregular food supply. Somehow all of these factors affect food habits at any given time. They determine the food habits of a group every day anew just as the amount of water supply and the nature of the riverbed determine from day to day the flow of the river, its constancy, or its change.

Food habits of a group, as well as such phenomena as the speed of production in a factory, are the result of a multitude of forces. Some forces support each other, some oppose each other. Some are driving forces, others restraining forces. Like the velocity of a river, the actual conduct of a group depends upon the level (for instance, the speed of production) at which these conflicting forces reach a state of equilibrium (my bolding). To speak of a certain culture pattern—for instance, the food habits of a group—implies that the constellation of these forces remains the same for a period or at least that they find their state of equilibrium at a constant level during that period.

Neither group "habits" nor individual "habits" can be understood sufficiently by a theory which limits its consideration to the processes themselves and conceives of the "habit" as a kind of frozen linkage, an "association" between these processes. Instead, habits will have to be conceived of as a result of forces in the organism and its life space, in the group and its setting. The structure of the organism, of the group, of the setting, or whatever name the field might have in the given case, has to be represented and the forces in the various parts of the field have to be analyzed if the processes (which might be either constant "habits" or changes) are to be understood scientifically. The process is but the epiphenomenon, the real object of study is the constellation of forces.

Therefore, to predict which changes in conditions will have what result we have to conceive of the life of the group as the result of specific constellations of forces within a larger setting. In other words, scientific predictions or advice for methods of change should be based on an analysis of the "field as a whole," including both its psychological and nonpsychological aspects.

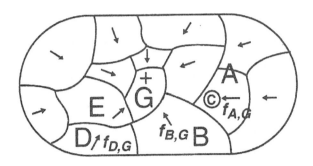

Figure 5.1
A positive central field of forces (Lewin, 1946, 1997, p349)

Force field analysis then, as mentioned earlier "to be done locally," is critical to unfreezing the current state. In field theory there are two types of forces, holding the current conditions in quasi-stasis or homeostasis.

Driving and Restraining Forces

The forces toward a positive, or away from a negative, valence can be called driving forces (see Figure 5.1, above). They lead to locomotion. These locomotions might be hindered by physical or social obstacles. Such barriers correspond to restraining forces. Restraining forces, as such, do not lead to locomotion, but they do influence the effect of driving forces (Lewin, 1946, 1997, 351).

Without the perspective of field theory, most try to bring about change by adding or increasing a driving force. This predictably leads to an increase in counter forces, and an elimination or reduction of any gains. As Lewin put it, "...a change brought about by adding forces in its direction leads to an increase in tension (Lewin, 1947, 1997, p324)." He elaborates in the following passage.

Two Basic Methods of Changing Level of Conduct

For any type of social management, it is of great practical importance that levels of quasi-stationary equilibria can be changed in either of two ways: by adding forces in the desired direction or by diminishing opposing forces. If a change... is brought about by increasing the forces toward... the secondary effects should be different from the case where the same change of level is brought about by diminishing the opposing forces.

...In the first case, the process... would be accomplished by a state of relatively high tension, in the second case, by a state of relatively low tension. Since increase of tension above a certain degree is likely to be paralleled by higher aggressiveness, higher emotionality, and lower constructiveness, it is clear that as a rule, the second method will be preferable to the high pressure method (my bolding) (Lewin, 1948, 1999, p280).

As usual, Lewin illustrated this phenomenon:

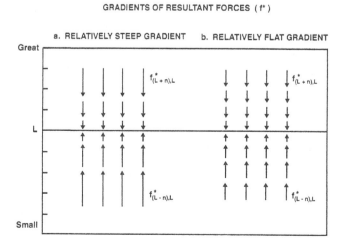

GRADIENTS OF RESULTANT FORCES (f*)

a. RELATIVELY STEEP GRADIENT   b. RELATIVELY FLAT GRADIENT

Figure 5.2
Gradients of resultant forces (Lewin, 1948, 1999, p280)

Push and people will push back. Push hard and the push back will be stronger. Reduce the restraining forces, and change will happen more smoothly and be more sustainable. Lewin's research and my own experience validate this theory. The question becomes then, what is the alternative to pushing? As he pointed out in the paper *Group Decision and Social Change* (Lewin, 1948, 1999, p273), Lewin's hypothesis was that the key to addressing and reducing restraining forces lay in group dynamics.

Individual Versus Group

The experiment does not try to bring about change of food habits by an approach to the individual, as such. Nor does it use the "mass approach" characteristic of radio and newspaper propaganda. Closer scrutiny shows that both the mass approach and the individual approach place the individual in a quasi-private, psychologically isolated situation with himself and his own ideas. Although he may physically be part of a group listening to a lecture, for example, he finds himself, psychologically speaking, in an "individual situation."

Even lecturing to a room full of employees, or conducting a public relations campaign for a change effort, is essentially approaching each person as an individual. While such efforts can play a role in disseminating information, they are inadequate for instilling lasting change in behaviors or beliefs. Lewin explains why: "One of the reasons why 'group carried changes' are more readily brought about seems to be the unwillingness of the individual to depart too far from group standards—he is likely to change only if the group changes (Lewin, 1948, 1999, p273)." With this in mind, the following excerpt from *Frontiers in Group Dynamics* (Lewin, 1947, 1997, p330) becomes a core principle of Lewin's approach to planned change.

Group Decision as a Change Procedure

The following example of a process of group decision concerns housewives living in a midwestern town, some of whom were exposed to a good lecture about the value of greater consumption of fresh milk and some of whom were involved in a discussion leading step by step to the decision to increase milk consumption. No high-pressure salesmanship was applied in fact, pressure was carefully avoided. The amount of time used was equal in the two groups. The change in milk consumption was checked after two and four weeks. Figure 5.3 (below) indicates the superiority of group decision.

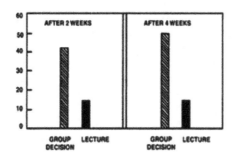

Percentage of mothers reporting an increase in the consumption of fresh milk after group decision and after lecture.

Figure 5.3
Percentage of mothers reporting an increase in the consumption of fresh milk (Lewin, 1948, 1999, p275)

Lewin replicated similar results time and again. As an aside, Lewin indeed exposed them to "a good lecture." Margaret

Mead was one of the lecturers. She recalled to Alfred Marrow with a chuckle of how she was brought into a similar food habits study as a "...prestige expert from Washington to express publicly my high approval of turnips—which had no effect at all (Marrow, 1969, p130)." Mead notes (again in Marrow, same page) that it was during the food habits studies, for which she had originally recruited Lewin, that the concept of "group decision" was formed.

Figure 5.4
A highly approved turnip

The food habits studies showed that people, when they are lectured to through traditional classroom methods, even though they are in a group are still in a primarily individual experience and isolated in their thinking. They only change as a group under such conditions if there happens to be a high occurrence of simultaneous individual change. Such a simultaneous individual change would require extraordinary circumstances. In contrast, when Lewin's participants in this and many other studies were encouraged to think out loud with each other *in a facilitated group discussion*, the group dynamics shifted *from a restraining force to a driving force*. The odds of individual change happening and sustaining go way up.

To be clear, this difference between group and individual methods is not magic. It doesn't come from simply locking a group in a room and leaving the quality of their discussion to chance. As Lewin put it: "The procedure of group decision in this experiment follows a step-by-step method designed a) to secure high involvement, and b) not to impede freedom of decision (Lewin, 1948, 1999, p271)." Lewin goes on, "It is possible that the success of group decision and particularly the permanency of the effect is, in part, due to the attempt to bring about a favorable decision by removing counterforces within the individuals rather than by applying outside pressure (Lewin, 1948, 1999, p281)." The counterforces within the individual can only diminish of their own volition. That is most likely to occur if people feel free to speak their minds, and if they are able to hear the opinions of their peers, whom they likely will trust more than an "expert." This holds true even if, like the mothers in the food habits study, they are strangers to each other at the beginning of the process.

Here we are seeing the shift away from "pushing" operationalized. As Lewin put it: "The group decision procedure which is used here attempts to avoid high pressure methods and is sensitive to resistance to change. In the experiment by Bavalas on changing production in factory work... for instance, no attempt was made to set the new production goal by majority vote because a majority vote forces some group members to produce more than they consider appropriate. These individuals are likely to have some inner resistance. Instead, a procedure was followed by which a goal was chosen on which everyone could agree fully (Lewin, 1948, 1999, p281)."

This rejection of "high pressure methods" became the foundation of the Knowledge Retrieval Implication Derivation or KRID model devised by Drs. Ron Lippitt and Charles Jung in the 1950s to assure the effective implementation of best practices. My father, brother Chris, and I have been applying KRID ever since. The step-by-step method is detailed in Appendix C.

Lewin explains the importance of group decision in planned change this way:

The experiments reported here cover but a few of the necessary variations. Although in some cases the procedure is relatively easily executed, in others it requires skill and presupposes certain general conditions. Managers rushing into a factory to raise production by group decisions are likely to encounter failure. In social management as in medicine there are no patent medicines and each case demands careful diagnosis. The experiments with group decision are nevertheless sufficiently advanced to clarify some of the general problems of social change.

We have seen that a planned social change may be thought of as composed of unfreezing, change of level, and freezing on the new level. In all three respects group decision has the general advantage of the group procedure.

If one uses individual procedures, the force field which corresponds to the dependence of the individual on a valued standard acts as a resistance to change. If, however, one succeeds in changing group standards, this same force field will tend to facilitate changing the individual and will tend to stabilize the individual conduct on the new group level (my bolding) (Lewin, 1947, 1997, p331).

Lewin's change method includes group decision as a reliable tool in changing the configuration of forces so as to drive and sustain change. The process leading to the group decision had to be active, not passive: "...there is a great difference in asking for a decision after a lecture or after a discussion. Since discussion involves active participation by the audience and a chance to express motivation towards different alternatives, the audience might be more ready to 'make up its mind,' that is to make a decision after a group discussion than after a lecture. A group discussion gives the leader a better indication of where the audience stands and what particular obstacles have to be overcome (Lewin, 1948, 1999, p273)."

In group decision, Lewin's theories regarding the social construction of reality and of intention/commitment/aspiration are validated. The first paragraph below is based on a study in which the researchers try to convince a group of college students to switch from white bread to whole wheat:

One reason why group decision facilitates change is illustrated by Willerman... When the change was simply requested the degree of eagerness varied greatly with the degree of personal preference for whole wheat. In case of group decision the eagerness seems to be relatively independent of personal preference the individual seems to act mainly as "group member."

A second factor favoring group decision has to do with the relation between motivation and action. A lecture and particularly a discussion may be quite effective in setting up motivations in the desired direction. Motivation alone, however, does not suffice to lead to change. That presupposes a link between motivation and action. This link is provided by the decision but it usually is not provided by lectures or even by discussions. This seems to be, at least in part, the explanation for the otherwise paradoxical fact that a process like decision which takes only a few minutes is able to affect conduct for many months to come. **The decision links motivation to action and, at the same time, seems to have a "freezing" effect which is partly due to the individual's tendency to "stick to his decision" and partly to the "commitment to a group."** The importance of the second factor would be different for a students' cooperative where the individuals remain together, for housewives from the same block who see each other once in a while, and for farm mothers who are not in contact with each other. The experiments show, however, that **even decisions concerning individual achievement can be effective which are made in a group setting of persons who do not see each other again** (my bolding)

(Lewin, 1947, 1997, p332).

If there is magic in Lewin's methods, this might be it. The effect of group decision, if participants really have a chance to dialogue with their peers and with people in positions of formal leadership, if they really have a chance, within reasonable limits, to make up their own minds, is an astonishingly reliable path to successful implementation of sustainable change. I was trained by my father in a basic process of group decision when I was 24, totally wet-behind-the-ears, dealing with understandably cynical elders in difficult manufacturing conditions, and it worked. I'm a living Lewinian research project, and I wouldn't want it any other way.

We'll explore Lewin's methods further, as well as my father's adaptations. Meanwhile, let us allow Lewin to bring this chapter to a close with the following nuggets of planned change wisdom:

A theory emerges that one of the causes of resistance to change lies in the relation between the individual and the value of group standards. This theory permits conclusions concerning the resistance of certain types of social equilibria to change, the unfreezing, moving, and freezing of a level, and the effectiveness of group procedures for changing attitudes or conduct.

The analytical tools used are equally applicable to cultural, economic, sociological, and psychological aspects of group life. They fit a great variety of processes such as production levels of a factory, a work-team and an individual worker; changes of abilities of an individual and of capacities of a country; group standards with and without cultural value; activities of one group and the interaction between groups, between individuals, and between individuals and groups.

The analysis concedes equal reality to all aspects of group life and to social units of all sizes (Lewin, 1947, 1997, p334).

Universal tools. I believe it. Let's go deeper now into Lewin's action research on group dynamics.

Chapter 6
Group Dynamics and Leadership

Group dynamics lay at the core of Lewin's social science and model of planned change. His research convinced him that "**...it is easier to change ideology or cultural habits by dealing with groups than with individuals** (my bolding) (Lewin, 1944, 1999, p289)."

Lewin's definition of what a group is was simple and pragmatic. "The essence of a group is not the similarity or dissimilarity of its members, but their interdependence (Lewin, 1940, 1997, p68.)" For example, a family is a group, even though the individual members may in many ways have more in common with people outside the group (other men, other women, other children) than with those within. The same holds true for any other type of group, such as work teams, sports teams, political parties, minorities, etc.

To belong, the individual must mesh the field of their own aspirations with those of the group. As Lewin put it, "The effect of group belongingness on the behavior of an individual can be viewed as the result of an overlapping situation: One situation corresponds to the person's own needs and goals: the other to the goals, rules, and values which exist for him as a group member. Adaptation of an individual to the group depends upon the avoidance of too great a conflict between the two sets of forces (Lewin, 1946, 1997, p360)."

"Peer pressure," as anyone knows who has worked in an organization, is a powerful force on the individual, whether at the executive or at the hourly level, and everywhere in between. Behave differently, such as working too hard or not hard enough, and you will be pushed and pulled back into place. Think differently and the same pressures will occur. As Lewin puts it: "An individual P may differ in his personal level of conduct (LP) from the level which represents group standards (LGr) by a certain amount n(LGr LP=n). Such a difference is permitted or encouraged in different cultures to different degrees. If the individual should try to diverge 'too much' from group standards he will find himself in increasing difficulties. He will be ridiculed, treated severely, and finally ousted from the group. Most individuals, therefore, stay pretty close to the standard of the groups they belong to or wish to belong to (Lewin, 1947, 1997, p328)."

Lewin's research thus indicates that morale and motivation are *systems issues*. That is, they are symptoms of the effect of the environment on the individual, more than the other way around: "How high a person will set his goal is deeply affected by the standards of the group to which he belongs, as well as by the standards of groups below and above him. Experiments with college students prove that, if the standards of a group are low, an individual will slacken his efforts and set his goals far below those he could reach. He will, on the other hand, raise his goals if the group standards are raised. In other words, both the ideals and the action of an individual depend upon the group to which he belongs and upon the goals and expectations of that group. **That the problem of individual morale is to a large extent a social psychological problem of group goals and group standards is thus clear**, even in those fields where the person seems to follow individual rather than group goals (my bolding)(Lewin, 1942, 1997, p87)."

As indicated in the last chapter, effectively conducted group dialogue, conscious goal and standard setting, and group decision are all drivers towards higher morale and measurable results. We are about to explore another important element in effective group dynamics, leadership (we will continue that exploration and address all of the above as applied to organization development in Chapters 10 and 13).

As mentioned, Lewin's hypothesis is that an effective group decision process generally results in increased willingness of individuals to consider new perspectives and adapt new behavior for the good of the group. Put one way, "...group decision provides a background of motivation where the individual is ready to cooperate as a member of the group more or less independent of his personal inclinations (Lewin, 1944, 1999, p289)." *This shift of group dynamics from a restraining force to a driving force is the critical lever needed to sustain changes in beliefs or behavior.* "Only by anchoring his own conduct in something as large, substantial, and superindividual as the culture of a group can the individual stabilize his new beliefs sufficiently to keep them immune from the day-by-day fluctuations of moods and influences to which he, as an individual, is subject (Lewin, 1945, 1997, p50)."

In other words, trying to change individuals without changing the social environment within which they live is like building one's house on sand. The group is the foundation that must be addressed, and even a newly formed group can hold the field of influence necessary for individual change. "Perhaps one might expect single individuals to be more pliable than groups of like-minded individuals. However, experience in leadership training, in changing of food habits, work production, criminality, alcoholism, prejudices—all seem to indicate that **it is usually easier to change individuals formed into a group than to change any one of them separately**. As long as group values are unchanged the individual will resist changes more strongly the further he is to depart from group standards. If the group standard itself is changed, the resistance which is due to the relation between individual and group standard is eliminated (my bolding) (Lewin, 1947, 1997, p329)."

What is this "effective" group process that can lead towards the desired results? This question brings us to some of Lewin's most striking and important research, the study of different "leadership atmospheres" on group behavior. His conclusion is clear. *Democratic principles, effectively applied, are critical to planned change and to the well-being of society.*

One democratic principle is that even though we play different roles in settings, including roles of formal authority, we all are equals in our basic humanity and want to be treated as such. With this in mind, in any intervention the principles begin with the conduct of the social scientist, or as it is stated in OD circles, with "the use of self." One aspect of "use of self" (not the only aspect) is how the social scientist relates to the people in the intervention. *In Lewin's mind, they must guide the process, but also engage as human peers.* As mentioned, the *diagnostic* or expert model can actually become a restraining force when conducting planned change. To influence a group, the social scientist must actually, even if only temporarily, become a peer with the group: "The normal gap between teacher and student, doctor and patient... can... be a real obstacle to acceptance of the advocated conduct. In other words, **in spite of whatever status differences there might be between them, the teacher and the student have to feel as members of one group in matters involving their sense of values.**

The chances for re-education seem to increase whenever a strong we-feeling is created (my bolding) (Lewin, 1945, 1997, p55)."

And why not? Whether or not one recognizes it, by joining the group in pursuit of the goals of the particular intervention, the social scientist truly is an interdependent member of the group in terms of whether the goals will be realized. By relating as a human being and not just as a role, the successful development of the "we-feeling" at least diminishes yet another restraining force (fear of the social scientist, the consultant, the stranger, the authority figure, etc.). Part of creating this "we-feeling," in Lewin's process, is another democratic principle, *freedom of expression:*

"When re-education involves the relinquishment of standards which are contrary to the standards of society at large (as in the case of delinquency, minority prejudices, alcoholism), **the feeling of group belongingness seems to be greatly heightened if the members feel free to express openly the very sentiments which are to be dislodged through re-education.** This might be viewed as another example of the seeming contradictions inherent in the process of re-education: Expression of prejudices against minorities or the breaking of rules of parliamentary procedures may in themselves be contrary to the desired goal. **Yet a feeling of complete freedom and a heightened group identification are frequently more important at a particular stage of re-education than learning not to break specific rules** (my bolding) (Lewin, 1945, 1997, p55)."

Contrary to some OD and HR practices, policing people out of saying what they think is not likely to bring sustained change and may actually have the opposite effect. This does not mean that anything goes, but it does mean that if the primary responsibility for thinking about what one is saying lies outside the individual, real change has not occurred. This brings us back to the importance of the group's role in the social construction and re-construction of reality, for which the fact-finding must be done "locally." In other words, only if you allow people to think for themselves and amongst themselves will reliable implementation and sustainable change occur.

As Lewin puts it: "This principle of in-grouping makes understandable why **complete acceptance of previously rejected facts can be achieved best through the discovery of these facts by the group members themselves.** Then, and frequently only then, do the facts become really *their* facts (as against other people's facts). An individual will believe facts he himself has discovered in the same way that he believes in himself or in his group. The importance of this fact-finding process for the group by the group itself has been recently emphasized with reference to re-education in several fields. **It can be surmised that the extent to which social research is translated into social action depends on the degree to which those who carry out this action are made a part of the fact-finding on which the action is to be based** (my bolding) (Lewin, 1945, 1997, p55)."

In *The Background of Conflict in Marriage* (Lewin, 1940, 1997, p69), Lewin sums up the dance between the individual and the group this way:

The Adaptation of the Individual to the Group

1. Group needs and individual freedom.

Belonging to a certain group does not mean that the individual must be in accord in every respect with the goals, regulations, and the style of living and thinking of the group. The individual has to a certain degree his own personal goals. He needs a sufficient space of free movement within the group to pursue those personal goals and to satisfy his individual wants. The problem of adaptation to, and successful living in, a group can be stated from the point of view of the individual in the following manner: How is it possible sufficiently to satisfy one's own individual needs without losing membership and status within the group? If the space of free movement of the individual within the group is too small, in other words, if his independence of the group is insufficient, the individual will be unhappy; too intense a frustration will force him to leave the group or will even destroy the group, if it limits the free movement of its members too severely.

2. Methods of adapting individual needs and group needs.

How the adjustment of the individual to the group has to be made depends upon the character of the group; the position of the individual within the group; the individual character of the person (especially the degree of independence he may need to be happy).

There are great differences in the manner in which individual and group needs are reconciled. The restrictions set up by the group may leave the individual much or little freedom. The restrictions may be based upon the democratic consent of the members of the group, or imposed by the will of an autocratic regime.

This brings us to the question of leadership in group dynamics, which Lewin and his research answer so well. During his University of Iowa years Lewin oversaw a series of experiments first by doctoral student Ron Lippitt, and then by Lippitt and post-doctoral fellow Ralph White. The initial study was of groups of boys and girls led by autocratic and democratic leaders. When Lewin observed White attempting to lead democratically during the second round of experiments, but doing so quite passively, he added a third category and dubbed it laissez-faire. As Lippitt tells it, "Kurt's observation of this, as he stood behind the burlap wall and operated the movie camera, led to an excited gleam in his eye as he perceived a basic gynotypic difference between the democratic pattern and what we labeled the laissez-faire pattern of leadership. So instead of correcting Ralph's style we moved it towards a more pure case of laissez-faire pattern and planned for other leaders to use the same role to get a more complete analysis of the dynamics of the difference. This shift is a good example of Kurt's creativity (Marrow, 1969, p124)."

The leadership styles are described in this table:

Authoritarian	Democratic	Laissez-faire
1. All determination of policy by the leader	1. All policies a matter of group discussion and decision, encouraged and assisted by the leader.	1. Complete freedom for group or individual decision, without any leader participation.
2. Techniques and activity steps dictated by the authority, one at a time, so that future steps were always uncertain to a large degree.	2. Activity perspective gained during first discussion period. General steps to group goal sketched, and where technical advice was needed the leader suggested two or three alternative procedures from which choice could be made.	2. Various materials supplied by the leader, who made it clear that he would supply information when asked. He took no other part in work discussions.
3. The leader usually dictated the particular work task and work companions of each member.	3. The members were free to work with whomever they chose, and the division of tasks was left up to the group.	3. Complete nonparticipation by leader.
4. The dominator was "personal" in his praise and criticism of the work of each member, but remained aloof from active group participation except when demonstrating. He was friendly or impersonal rather than openly hostile.	4. The leader was "objective" or "fact-minded" in his praise and criticism, and tried to be a regular group member in spirit without doing too much of the work.	4. Very infrequent comments on member activities unless questioned, and no attempt to participate or interfere with the course of events.

Figure 6.1

Authoritarian, democratic and laissez-faire leadership styles (Lewin, 1939, 1999, p229)

The results are as relevant today as they were at the time. Lippitt and White described the initial experiment later in their 1960 book, *Autocracy and Democracy: An Experimental Inquiry:* "A small number of eleven-year-old children met after school to make masks and carry on other activities. They were divided into two groups of five each. They were led by the same person and met eleven times, but with one batch he played a 'democratic' role and created a democratic atmosphere and with the other he played an 'autocratic' role. Five observers took continuous notes on the behavior of the leader and the children…the groups behaved similarly at the onset, they rapidly became different, so that in later meetings the contrast was striking. In brief, there was far more quarreling and hostility in the autocratically led group, and far more friendliness and group spirit in the one democratically led. The children in the autocratic group picked on scapegoats and showed other behavior that seemed too similar to certain contemporary dictatorships to be mere coincidence (Marrow, 1969, p125)."

In other words, you get what you give. Change the leadership pattern in a group or a system, and you change the system. Democratic principles lead to higher morale and importantly, also to high productivity. Perhaps surprisingly, laissez-faire (passive leadership), leads to high tension and conflict in the system, and low productivity. Autocracy, like democracy, although clearly inferior in the long run, at least gets short-term results. Based on the experiments overseen by Lewin, laissez-faire is actually the least desirable of the three. My own experience and that of my father and my associates indicates that *while having an autocratic boss is feared by many, overly passive bosses are far more prevalent.* Recent research documented in the *British Journal of Management* supports this hypothesis: "The results showed that laissez-faire leadership behaviour was the most prevalent destructive leadership behaviour… while tyrannical leadership behaviour was the least prevalent destructive leadership behaviour (Aasland et al, 2010, p1)."

Based on this evolving series of experiments with adults leading boys and girls groups autocratically, democratically (with clear authority by the leader combined with group dialogue and decisions), and passively (or laissez-faire), Lewin concluded that: "**Autocracy is imposed on the individual. Democracy he has to learn** (my bolding) (Lewin, 1939, 1997, p66)." The kids knew quickly how to cope with an authoritarian leader. They had to learn how to participate in a democratic group. They were lost under a laissez-faire leader. When children were switched from one group to another, they quickly adapted to the norms of the new group, reinforcing Lewin's beliefs about group dynamics and peer pressure.

The implications for leadership and group dynamics are profound. "Scapegoating" or "incidents of aggression" were as prevalent in the laissez-faire group as in the authoritarian group, and much less prevalent in the democratically led group. This held true even when the leadership styles were switched for the same groups of boys. Most people, including many OD professionals, demonize authoritarian leadership. Lewin's research indicates that *"nice" leaders that are too passive actually cause as much chaos in group relations and have less success in terms of task output.* Lewin's democratic leader, clearly in charge while allowing significant task influence, got the best task and group relations outcomes. As Lewin put it: "In contrast to both democratic and autocratic groups, the laissez-faire group, where the leader keeps hands off, shows only sporadic flare-ups of group planning or of long-range individual projects. The work morale of such a group is very low compared with either that of the democratic or the autocratic group—an indication of the importance of definite goals for group morale (Lewin, 1942, 1997, p89)." Again, we will explore the implications for OD more in Chapters 10 and 13.

Lewin adds this interesting perspective: "Autocracy, democracy, and laissez-faire should be perceived as a triangle. In many respects, autocracy and democracy are similar: They both mean leadership as against the lack of leadership of laissez-faire; they both mean discipline and organization as against chaos. Along other lines of comparison, democracy and laissez-faire are similar. They both give freedom to the group members in so far as they create a situation where the members are acting on their own motivation rather than being moved by forces induced by an authority in which they have no part (Lewin, 1944, 1999, p286)." In other words, democracy is the only corner of the triangle that combines leadership *and* freedom (Figure 6.2, facing page).

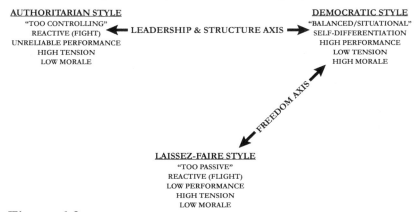

Figure 6.2
Lewin leadership style triangle (Crosby, 2020)

Compared to the other two patterns, effective democratic leadership boosts morale: "Later Lippitt and White studied four new (boys) clubs with other leaders. They included a third atmosphere, namely that of laissez-faire, and exposed the same children successively to a number of atmospheres. On the whole, the results bear out those of Lippitt. They show a striking difference between laissez-faire and democracy very much in favor of democracy. They show further two types of reaction in the autocratic groups, one characterized by aggression, the second by apathy...

There have been few experiences for me as impressive as seeing the expression in children's faces change during the first day of autocracy. The friendly, open, and co-operative group full of life, became within a short half-hour a rather apathetic-looking gathering without initiative (Lewin, 1939, 1997, p66)."

Lewin concludes that statement by noting the following: "The change from autocracy to democracy seemed to take somewhat more time than from democracy to autocracy," and then this, which bears repeating, "Autocracy is imposed on the individual. Democracy he has to learn (Lewin, 1939, 1997, p66)."

In other words, most people know how to bark orders, and most know how to cope with authoritarianism through acquiescence or through overt or covert resistance. Effective democracy takes more skill and responsibility. Both leaders and followers have to learn how to be active participants in a democracy. Since Lewin's methods of planned change are grounded in democratic principles, training in the application of those principles became part of his strategy.

Lewin and his associates used three methods to test their hypothesis that group dynamics (as determined by leadership patterns) not individual differences was the critical variable influencing behavior:

1. They moved individual group members and documented their resultant behaviors (below):

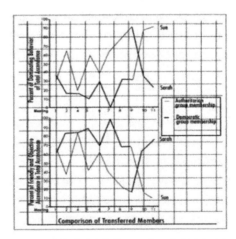

After the eighth meeting Sue was transferred from the democratic to the autocratic group, Sarah from the autocratic to the democratic group. The overt character of both children changed according to the atmosphere.

Figure 6.3
Transfer of children (Lewin, 1939, 1997, p65)

As you can see, the overt behavior of both children changed according to the group atmosphere. Lewin notes, "One may ask whether these results are not due merely to individual differences. A number of facts rule out this explanation, although of course individual differences also play a role. Of particular interest was the transfer of one of the children from the autocratic group to the democratic group, and of another from the democratic to the autocratic one... the behavior of the children mirrored very quickly the atmosphere of the group in which they moved (Lewin, 1939, 1997, p65)."

2. They rotated the leaders so that every group experienced each leadership style. Again, the behavioral responses of the children were predictable and consistent. Of interest were spikes in aggression as each group moved from autocratic leadership to either of the other patterns: "First of all, there are sudden outbursts of aggression which occurred on the days of transition from a repressed autocratic atmosphere to the much freer atmosphere of democracy or laissez-faire... The boys behaved just as if they had previously been in a state of bottled-up tension, which could not show itself overtly as long as the repressive influence of the autocrat was felt, but which burst out unmistakably when that pressure was removed (Lewin, 1939, 1999, p237)." Lewin attributes this not just to modeling by the authoritarian leader, which was a factor, but primarily to the level of tension experienced in the group (see Figure 6.4, next page):

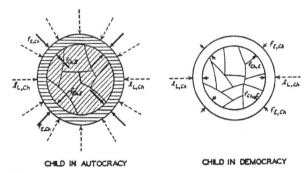

CHILD IN AUTOCRACY   CHILD IN DEMOCRACY

Leader pressure and child tension. In the authoritarian situation the leader makes six times as many directing approaches ($l_{L,Ch}$) to the child member as in the democratic situation. This creates social pressure (equivalent to forces $f_{E,Ch}$ of the environment on the child) and therefore a higher state of tension in the child in the autocratic group: This tension demands some sort of outlet toward the environment (equivalent to forces $f_{Ch,E}$).

Figure 6.4

Leader pressure and child tension (Lewin, 1941, 1999, p244)

The rates of aggression after transition fell off considerably over time in the democratic group, less so in the laisse-faire atmosphere, where there was a different kind of tension—that of tension over lack of direction.

3. They periodically pulled the leaders out of the rooms. This had an impact on both aggression and productivity, with marked differences based on the leadership pattern of the group. Regarding aggression Lewin reported the following: "The children in the autocratic group ganged together not against their leader, but against one of the children and treated him so badly that he ceased coming to the club (Lewin, 1939, 1997, p64)."

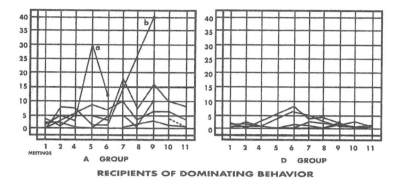

Figure 6.5
Recipients of dominating behavior (Lewin, 1939, 1999, p232)

No such scapegoating occurred in the democratic group. Interestingly, the boys who got ganged up on and "scapegoated" by the group, had been "dominating" of their peers while the autocratic leader had been in the room (Figure 6.5, above).

Interaction and Circular Causal Processes

The scapegoats A and B who received much dominating behavior themselves showed much dominating behavior. This indicates a close relation between being attacked and attacking. This relation has the character of a circular causal process: the attack of A against B increases B's readiness to attack; the resultant attacks of B raise A's readiness, etc. (Lewin, 1947, 1997, p319).

While the effect on aggression holds implications both for politics and for healthy group dynamics, the effect on productivity is perhaps of even more importance in terms of implications for planned change and organization development. *The children in the autocratic and laissaz-faire groups got very little done when the leader left the room. The children in the democratic groups continued to produce.* This was true when the leaders were pulled from the room, or when the same children were led by a new pattern of leadership.

In *Time Perspective and Morale*, Lewin offers this explanation:

"These groups... showed very striking differences during periods when the leader left. Whereas the work morale of the democratic group was sustained at a high level, that of the autocratic group fell rapidly. In a short time, the latter group ceased entirely to produce..."

The organization of work, like any other aspect of the organization of the autocratic group, is based on the leader. It is he who determines the policy of the group it; is he who sets the specific goals of action for the members within the group. That means that the goals of the individual as well as his action as a group member are "induced" by the leader. It is the leader's power-field which keeps the individual going, which determines his work morale, and which makes the group an organized unit. In the democratic group, on the contrary, every member has had a hand in determining the policy of the group; every member has helped to lay out the plans. As a result, each is more "we-centered" and less "ego-centered" than the member of the autocratic group. Because the group goes ahead under its own steam, its work morale does not flag as soon as the power-field of the leader is eliminated...

In the democratic group, "acceptance" of the group goal by the member means taking it over and making it one's own goal. The readiness to do so, in the latter case, is partly based on the time perspective of the individual in the past, that is, he himself has participated in setting up that goal and now he feels his individual responsibility in carrying it through (Lewin, 1942, 1997, p88).

In addition, Lewin notes that, "In the autocracy instead of a cooperative attitude, a hostile and highly personal attitude became prevalent... in the autocratic group the children were matter of fact, less co-operative, and submissive toward their equals, but more submissive to their superior... This has a rather clear effect on the amount of individuality. In our experiment every individual in the democracy showed a relatively greater individuality, having some field of his own in spite of the greater 'we' feeling among them, or perhaps because of it. In the autocratic group on the contrary the children all had a low status without much individuality (Lewin, 1939, 1997, p64)."

In other words, the children in the democratic group had a much higher sense of ownership and responsibility for the task and did not have to be closely supervised to remain productive; group dynamics about which most organizations dream.

Lewin concludes, "...the group the person is a part of, and the culture in which he lives, determine to a very high degree his behavior and character (Lewin, 1939, 1997, p66)."

Change the culture, change the individual. Create a culture based on democratic principles and you can improve implementation, morale, and productivity. Therein lies the foundation for planned change. The implications for organization development are huge. The political implications are just as important. Let us now turn the lens of Lewin's universal social science in that direction.

Chapter 7
Social Science and Politics

Robert Sears, whose agency collaborated with Lewin in Iowa, noted the following about Lewin's passion for democracy: "The autocratic way he insisted on democracy was a little spectacular. There was nothing to criticize – but one couldn't help noticing the fire and the emphasis (Marrow, 1969, p127)." Small wonder, given Lewin's firsthand experience of WWI, of Nazism in Germany, and of anti-Semitism even before the rise of Hitler. Lewin was in a race against time to have advances in social science catch up with advances in technology in time to keep us from annihilating ourselves. "There is no hope for creating a better world without a deeper scientific insight into the function of leadership, of culture, and of other essentials of group life. Social life shall have to be managed much more consciously than before if man shall not destroy man (Lewin, 1943, 1999, p334)."

Lewin was idealistic, but not naively so. He believed that a democratic leader had to assert authority, and that democracy could not afford to tolerate intolerance.

"The democratic leader is no less a leader and, in a way, has not less power than the autocratic leader. There are soft and tough democracies as well as soft and tough autocracies; and a tough democracy is likely to be more rather than less democratic. The difference between autocracy and democracy is an honest, deep difference, and an autocracy with a democratic front is still an autocracy...

It is particularly interesting to consider what might be called an efficient 'tough democracy.'

The gospel of inefficiency of democracies has been preached and believed not only in Nazi Germany. We ourselves are somewhat surprised to see the democratic countries execute this war rather efficiently. When Lippitt's first study (1940) showed the beneficial effects which the democratic atmosphere has on the overt character of the member, how it changes his behavior from hostility to friendliness, from egocentrism to we-feeling, and to an objective matter-of-fact attitude, the argument was frequently presented that these results may hold in the friendly settings of a boys' club, but that the advantages of the democratic atmosphere would not stand up in a tough situation such as an industry requiring high efficiency (Lewin, 1944, 1999, p287)."

Lewin believed that for democracy to work, freedom has to have limits, and the leadership must enforce those limits: "A democratic world order does not require or even favor cultural uniformity all over the world. The parallel to democratic freedom for the individual is cultural pluralism for groups. But any democratic society has to safeguard against misuse of individual freedom by the gangster or—politically speaking —the 'intolerant.' Without establishing to some degree the principle of tolerance, of equality of rights, in every culture the 'intolerant' culture will always be endangering a democratic world organization. Intolerance against intolerant cultures is therefore a prerequisite to any organization of permanent peace (Lewin, 1943, 1997, p36.)"

The "intolerant" know no boundaries. The boundaries must be set for them or, as Edwin Friedman put it, they will spread like a virus. Empathy for the "rights" of the intolerant will only be used against the empathetic: "The form of human colonization that functions most similarly to a virus or a malignant cell is the totalitarian nation. No human entity is more invasive. The totalitarian nation is equally invasive of the lives of its citizens and the space of its neighbors...The two are linked... by the absence of self-regulation; they make no attempt to regulate their drive in either direction. They infect what they touch and they seek to replicate their own being by taking over any host they 'occupy.' They certainly do not know when to quit. It is this same lack of self-regulation and the inner integrity required for self-definition that makes totalitarian states as notoriously untrustworthy of agreements and treaties as a crime syndicate…and this brings us back… to the irrelevance of empathy in the face of a relentless force (Friedman, 1999, p148)."

Lewin would certainly have agreed. In several papers he used the recent history of Germany as a case study for studying democracy and contrasting it with totalitarianism:

"It has been one of the tragedies of the German Republic that the democratically minded people who were in power immediately after the war confused democracy with 'being unpolitical'…It was a tragedy that they did not know that 'intolerance against the intolerant' is…essential for maintaining and particularly for establishing a democracy…above all it was a tragedy that they did not know that strong leadership and an efficient positive use of the political power by the majority is an essential aspect of democracy. Instead, Germany congratulated herself on having 'the freest Constitution in the world' because technically even a small minority gets its proportional representation in the parliament. Actually, this set-up led to dozens of political parties and to the permanent domination of the majority by a minority group…(Lewin, 1943, 1997, p37)."

Appeasement of the more radical elements of society failed, even though the majority favored peace: "Even in Germany right after the last war the proportion of the population which turned to pacifism was probably larger than the group which started immediately to build for revenge…(Lewin, 1943, 1997, p36)."

Lewin was a visionary about global peace and how to get there, but he was no proponent of always turning the other cheek:

Friendliness is no appropriate response to an aggressor. In recent years we have seen in world politics how undignified, morally distasteful and unwise is the policy of appeasing an aggressor. It is both shameful and stupid to talk to a man who is determined to destroy you. For the enemy such friendly talk means only that you are either too weak or too cowardly to fight him. We should not be mistaken about the following point either: the onlooker, who is not yet prejudiced, might be won over and brought to sympathize with an individual or a group of people who fight back with all their power against an aggressor, while he will show very little sympathy for people who bow to an insult. Britain has felt the truth of this simple observation rather keenly within the last two years.

I hope that Jews in America will recognize this truth before it is too late. There are now many among us who adopt the attitude of "talking things over" and "getting together" without the necessary discrimination. This attitude is entirely correct and advisable with friends and neutrals, but not if we have to deal with groups which have made up their mind to destroy us.

The Jew will have to realize, and he will have to realize it fast, that in fighting Nazis and their allies it does not pay to be polite. There is only one way to fight an enemy, and this is to return blow for blow, to strike back immediately, and if possible, harder. Jews can expect to get active help from others only if they themselves show that they have the courage and the determination to stand up for a fight of self-defense (Lewin, 1939,1997, p120).

Fortunately, when democracies take a stand, there is strong evidence that the same democratic principles that motivated the groups of children in Lewin's experiments to take it upon themselves to keep working also motivates armies made up of democratic citizens. Here I turn to Victor Hansen, author of *The Soul of Battle*, who makes the case that the democratic culture, when necessary, produces a superior fighting force:

"Democracies, I think—if the cause, if the commanding general, if the conditions of time and space take on their proper meaning—for a season can produce the most murderous armies from the most unlikely of men, and do so in the pursuit of something spiritual rather than the mere material...

Theban hoplites, Union troops, and American GIs, this book argues, were ideological armies foremost, composed of citizen-soldiers who burst into their enemy's heartland because they believed it was a just and very necessary thing to do. The commanders who lead them encouraged that ethical zeal, made them believe there was a real moral difference between Theban democracy and Spartan helotage, between a free Union and a slave-owning South, and between a democratic Europe and a nightmarish Nazi continent. This study is more an essay on the ethical nature of democracies at war than a purely military history of three epic marches for freedom, for it claims that on rare occasions throughout the ages there can be a soul, not merely a spirit, in the way men battle (Hanson, 1999, p5 and p12)."

Nonetheless, sustaining democracy through the willingness to fight is not the most desirable path. Even if it were, technological advances in the destructiveness of war will eventually make it unsustainable. Over-dependence on the military to sustain democracy also raises the specter of the "military-industrial complex" becoming an unhealthy influence, as per President Eisenhower's warning, and as many of founders of the United States feared. As James Madison put it in 1787 at the Constitutional Convention in Philadelphia, "A standing military force, with an overgrown Executive will not long be safe companions to liberty...The means of defense against foreign danger, have been always the instruments of tyranny at home. Among the Romans it was a standing maxim to excite a war, whenever a revolt was apprehended. Throughout all Europe, the armies kept up under the pretext of defending, have enslaved the people (Kohn, 1975)." Promoting democratic principles so as to decrease armed conflicts is a far better path.

In Lewin's words: "Throughout history, political geniuses have arisen who have been masters in group management, such as Napoleon or Hitler. The only hope, however, for a permanent foundation of successful social management, and particularly for a permanent democratic society of the common man, is a social management based to a high degree on a scientific insight which is accessible to many (Lewin, 1943, 1999, p334)." If we are to achieve a better world based on democratic principles, it will only happen through clear-eyed determined effort: "It is a fallacy to assume that people, if left alone, follow a democratic pattern in their group life. Such an assumption would not even hold for people living in a democratic society (Lewin, 1943, 1997, p37)." If a high percentage of leaderless work teams in the United States erode into autocratic or laissez-faire leadership patterns, as happened at Alcoa's Addy Washington magnesium plant (where my father was hired to put front line supervision and democratic principles back into the system) and numerous other well-intentioned organizations (such as the Uddevalla Volvo plant in Sweden), what are the odds a non-democratic country will transform overnight into effective democratic principles? It's perhaps more likely that a democratic country, by appeasing the "intolerant," will allow its democracy to erode. As mentioned, people adapt to authoritarianism fast, while democracy must be learned anew by each generation:

"In democracy, as in any culture, the individual acquires the cultural pattern by some type of 'learning.' Normally such learning occurs by way of growing up in that culture... experiments indicate that autocracy can be 'imposed upon a person.' That means the individual might 'learn' autocracy by adapting himself to a situation forced upon him from outside. **Democracy cannot be imposed upon a person; it has to be learned by a process of voluntary and responsible participation** (my bolding) (Lewin, 1943, 1997, p38)."

With that in mind, Lewin pondered the enormous planned culture change effort that lay ahead for both Germany and Japan. In his article *Cultural Reconstruction* Lewin wrote, "Building a world of peace which will be worth at least the name 'better than before' includes many problems: political, economic, and cultural. Each of them is loaded with difficulties. Yet all of them have to be considered together and attacked together as interdependent aspects of one dynamic field if any successful step forward is to be achieved (Lewin, 1943, 1997, p35)." As usual, his writing on the subject has implications for other topics, including education, social justice, and OD, and I have spread excerpts into the chapters ahead.

Lewin was a consultant to the war department, so the people who crafted the Marshall Plan were at least in his orbit of relationships. The plan, perhaps the most ambitious and successful cultural change effort in human history, was drafted and implemented after his death. I have found no documentation thus far that directly proves Lewin's influence on reconstruction, but the simultaneous success in Germany, Japan, and Italy makes his influence seem likely. We need look no further than the post-civil war reconstruction here in the United States, where the forces of intolerance were allowed to re-establish their power, to know that successful reconstruction is easier said than done.

Lewin was a passionate advocate that the lessons of post WWI Germany be learned and learned well before attempting reconstruction of the German culture after WWII:

"After the last war the reactionary forces in Germany, although driven under cover, were permitted to 'get away with it.' Being a socially well-knit group, they soon started to come back step by step and to take their revenge in the extreme form of Hitlerism. I cannot see any hope of more than superficial change after the present war if the German people are prevented from getting rid in a very thorough fashion of a large group which has developed to perfection the most ruthless methods of suppression...

The German move towards democracy after the last war did not fail because the so-called German Revolution of 1918 was too chaotic, but because the overthrow of the Kaiser was bloodless and did not reach deep enough. It did not reach deep enough socially to remove certain sections of the population from power, and it did not reach deep enough culturally to remove the idea of democracy from its identification with individualistic freedom of the laissez-faire type (Lewin, 1943, 1997, p42)."

While offering sound advice, such as working with and engaging the people of Germany and of Europe in a massive cultural action research project instead of simply imposing solutions on them, Lewin was only guardedly optimistic about the outcome of reconstruction: "We will have to avoid the naive belief that people 'left alone' will choose democracy. We have to avoid building our plans on 'hatred of the enemy', but we have to also avoid building our plans on wishful thinking and blindness against reality. We should know, for instance, that we have to deal in Germany with a set-up where month after month, day after day, six to seven thousand unwanted women and children are killed in central slaughter houses in occupied territories, and where thousands of people must have grown accustomed to doing such jobs. American newspapers seem to play down such unpleasant truths probably because they wish to prevent a peace based on hatred. Actually, this procedure defies its purpose because in politics as in education a successful action has to be based on a full knowledge of reality (Lewin, 1943, 1997, p 39)."

Lewin was a firm believer that objective discussion of the facts, no matter how disturbing, was the way forward: "Democracy and Judaism have nothing to fear from truth and fact finding, but they have much to gain by them (Lewin, 1944, 1999, p263)."

Like the founders of the United Sates, he believed in the promise of reason, saw it as a critical underpinning of democracy and social science, and thought it was the job of both parents and education to instill it from the beginning of life: "**To believe in reason is to believe in democracy, because it grants to the reasoning partners a status of equality.** It is therefore not an accident that not until the rise of democracy at the time of the American and French Revolutions was the 'goddess' of reason enthroned in modern society. And again, it is not an accident that the very first act of modern Fascism in every country has been officially and vigorously to dethrone this goddess and instead to make emotions and obedience the all-ruling principles in education and life from kindergarten to death (my bolding) (Lewin, 1939, 1997, p67)."

Indeed, Lewin believed changing the authoritarian nature of the educational system in Germany, and even of the family, was essential to real and lasting culture change following WWII. Lewin advocated that adults should treat the "…child as a thinking person. A child in a democratic atmosphere from his earliest days is not treated as an object but, as a person, is given explanation and reasons for the events in his surroundings, and especially for necessary limitations of his freedom; he is given the right to make himself understood, to ask questions, and to tell 'his side of the story.' He is given the chance to make a choice and to make his own decisions wherever this is reasonably possible. Such a child will build a better emotional basis for social living and will be prepared to shoulder responsibilities when he becomes mature enough to play with other children his age (Lewin, 1941, 1999, p322)."

Last but not least, Lewin used his experience in Germany to study minority relations in a hostile environment, or what might be called racial tension today, and the tendencies of autocratic leaders to scapegoat minorities:

It should be understood that any underprivileged minority is preserved as such by the more privileged majority...Today again, it can easily be shown how any increase or decrease in the economic difficulties of the majority increases or decreases the pressure upon the Jewish minority. This is one of the reasons why Jews everywhere are necessarily interested in the welfare of the majority among whom they live.

It has been recognized long ago that the basis of anti-Semitism is partly the need of the majority for a scapegoat. Frequently in modern history it is not the majority as such but an autocratic group ruling the majority which needs the scapegoat as a means of distracting the masses. The most striking recent example is Mussolini's sudden attack on the Italian Jews against whom practically no anti-Semitic feeling had existed before. The same Mussolini, who but a few years ago was favorably disposed toward Zionism, found it wise to follow Hitler's example, or he may have been forced by Hitler to do so. Certainly nothing in the conduct of Italian Jewry has given the slightest cause for this change. Here again, the need of the majority or of their ruling elite alone has determined the fate of the Jewish community...

Anti-Semitism cannot be stopped by the good behavior of the individual Jew, because it is not an individual, but a social problem.

How little relation exists between Jewish conduct and anti-Semitism is well illustrated by the way the majority shifts its official reasons for maltreatment. For hundreds of years the Jews have been persecuted for religious reasons. Today racial theories serve as pretext. The reasons are easily changed according to whatever seems to be the most efficient argument at the moment...in this country one of the most influential associations of manufacturers is working with two types of pamphlets. One of these pamphlets, used when a group of workers or middle-class people are approached, pictures the Jew as a capitalist and as an international banker. But if the same propagandist speaks to an audience of manufacturers, he uses a pamphlet which pictures the Jews as communists.

The Jew answering accusations should realize that they are but a surface, below which deeper social problems are hidden even in those cases when the argument is put forth in good faith. The need of the majority for a scapegoat grows out of tension, e.g., from an economic depression. Scientific experiments prove that this need is particularly strong in tensions which are due to an autocratic regime. No "logical" argument will destroy these basic forces (Lewin, 1939, 1997, p118).

I leave it to the reader to draw conclusions about parallels between the forces Lewin was fighting until the time of his death, and political conditions today. I'm sure you will agree that there is still much work to be done. I am convinced that Lewinian theory grounded in democratic principles still offers a sound foundation for the betterment, and perhaps the political salvation, of humanity.

Let us now move on to more of Lewin's beliefs about education.

Chapter 8
Education, Re-education and Training

"We are slowly coming to realize that all education is group work (Lewin, 1943, 1999, p334)." Certainly that is true in primary education, most types of effective training, and in what Lewin termed "re-education," which is the process of helping individuals change how they think and behave in relation to issues such as race and role (especially how to effectively lead and how to effectively follow).

Lewin saw education as a reflection of the broader culture in which it resides, and as an influence in promulgating or changing that culture.

"Education is in itself a social process...Education tends to develop certain types of behavior, certain kinds of attitudes ...there exists a general cultural atmosphere...Those who have had the opportunity to observe closely enough the behavior of school teachers (for instance, in Germany between 1917 and 1933, especially in the period 1931-1933) could easily see how even small changes in the general political situation affected, almost from day to day, not only the ideals which they taught, but also the educational methods which they employed (such as the type and frequency of punishment, the amount of drill, and the degree of freedom and independence in learning). Times of political change show very impressively the high degree to which education, in nearly all of its aspects, depends upon the social structure of the group. *It seems to be easier for society to change education than for education to change society* (Lewin, 1936, 1997, p16)."

True to form, Lewin saw the same dynamics everywhere. In his eyes, more important than the content for the most part, is the educational process itself. If you are teaching a class on democracy, yet suppressing dialogue and valuing compliance, memorization, and drill over critical thinking, you are actually teaching authoritarianism through your actions with more lasting effect than you are teaching democracy through your words. Regardless of the content, the process of teaching either reinforces democratic principles (active engagement and influence), or it does not:

"...for educating future citizens, no talk about democratic ideals can substitute for a democratic atmosphere in the school. The character and the cultural habits of the growing citizen are not so much determined by what he says as by what he lives (Lewin, 1944, 1999, p290)."

Lewin's research clearly differentiated between active and passive participation, with active participation consistently yielding superior results. As noted earlier, when he was in a teaching or group leadership role, he walked his own talk, encouraging his students into active dialogue even while at the stodgy University of Berlin, where such behavior was far out of the norm: "**Lecturing is a procedure by which the audience is chiefly passive. The discussion, if conducted correctly, is likely to lead to a much higher degree of involvement** (my bolding) (Lewin, 1948, 1999, p271)."

Through group dynamics, Lewin found that the social construction of reality could be shifted, and hence individual beliefs and values could be opened to influence. Active group participation, shifting the group from a restraining force to a driving force, was essential to the difficult goals of re-education: "The re-educative process affects the individual in three ways. It changes his *cognitive structure*, the way he sees the physical and social world, including all his facts, concepts, beliefs, and expectations. It modifies his *valances and values,* and these embrace both his attractions and aversions to groups and group standards, his feelings in regard to status differences, and his reactions to sources of approval or disapproval. And it affects *motoric action*, involving the degree of the individual's control over his physical and social movements (Lewin, 1945, 1997, p50)."

Through re-education, which of course is a form of training, Lewin was a pioneer in the reduction and elimination of strongly held beliefs, such as prejudice, and to instilling democratic principles in leaders and their subordinates. Although they never met, Lewin's efforts to create change through what came to be called experiential education paralleled American educator John Dewey. Indeed, two of Lewin's most important associates, Leland Bradford and Ken Benne, "…were both students of Dewey's philosophy of education (Bennis, Benne and Chin, 1961, p45)."

In Lewin's mind, experiential learning became critical to re-education. That is, learning through an active experience that impacts the *cognitive structure, valences and values*, and *motoric action*, and through facilitated reflection on that experience. In his paper *Conduct, Knowledge, and Acceptance of New Values* Lewin made it clear that random experience is not enough to assure learning, and hence is not the same thing as "experiential learning":

"The difficulties encountered in efforts to reduce prejudices or otherwise to change the social outlook of the individual have led to a realization that re-education cannot be merely a rational process. We know that lectures or other similarly abstract methods of transmitting knowledge are of little avail in changing his subsequent outlook and knowledge. We might be tempted, therefore, to think that what is lacking in these methods is first-hand experience...

Even extensive first-hand experience does not automatically create correct concepts (knowledge).

For thousands of years man's everyday experience with falling objects did not suffice to bring him to a correct theory of gravity. A sequence of very unusual, man-made experiences, so-called experiments, which grew out of the systematic search for the truth were necessary to bring about a change from less adequate to more adequate concepts. To assume that first-hand experience in the social world would automatically lead to the formation of correct concepts or to the creation of adequate stereotypes seems therefore unjustifiable (Lewin, 1945, 1997, p48-55)."

Apples had been falling since the dawn of time! It took the accumulated knowledge of humanity up to the right moment combined with the inspiration of Sir Isaac Newton to formulate a scientifically valid theory of gravity.

Neither Lewin, nor I, nor my OD customers think we have that much time! Re-education must work relatively fast. It must also reach deep within the individual. To do so and to have it last requires a process in which the individual willingly rethinks their own beliefs and behaviors. Like the groups of children under democratic leadership, the individual must reach a point of taking responsibility for their own learning. If behavior is only enforced from outside, re-education has failed. As Lewin put it: "Re-education is frequently in danger of only reaching the official system of values, the level of verbal expression and not of conduct; it may result in merely heightening the discrepancy between the super-ego (the way I ought to feel) and the ego (the way I really feel), and thus give the individual a bad conscience. Such a discrepancy leads to a state of high emotional tension, but seldom to correct conduct. It may postpone transgressions, but it is likely to make the transgressions more violent when they occur.

A factor of great importance in bringing about a change in sentiment is the degree to which the individual becomes actively involved in the problem. Lacking this involvement, no objective fact is likely to reach the status of a fact for the individual concerned and therefore influence his social conduct (my bolding) (Lewin, 1945, 1997, p52)."

If people are simply lectured at – moralized at by a critical authority figure – then all they are likely to learn is to watch what they say around the authorities. Such approaches increase polarization instead of decreasing it. Conflict goes underground, where it simmers. To foster real and lasting change the individual, in concert with the group, must be facilitated in doing genuine action research on themselves. They must test beliefs, old and new, and test new behaviors through dialogue and interaction. When done effectively, Lewin's methods achieved (and still achieve) reliable and dramatic results:

"**Experiments in leadership training have shown that it is even possible... to transform highly autocratic leaders of long standing within a short time into efficient democratic leaders** (my bolding) (Lewin, 1943, 1997, p41)."

The following is one example from Lewin's work in industry, which we will explore in more depth in Chapter 10:

"An example of a successful change in ideology and social behavior is the retraining of relatively autocratic recreation leaders into excellent democratic leaders, as carried out by Bavelas. These leaders had followed their method of handling groups for five to seven years. **The change took place within three weeks**. It was brought about partly by observation of other leaders and a detailed discussion of the various possibilities of the leader's reactions to a multitude of situations arising from group life. In this way, the cognitive structure of the field 'leader behavior' became much more finely differentiated; the individual became sensitized. The motivational change from skepticism to enthusiasm for democratic procedure cannot be discussed here in detail. It came about, in part, through the thrill of experiencing what a democratic group-life can do to children, and through the realization that one is able to create such an atmosphere. The preceding years had been for these people a period of low morale, of dissatisfaction with the insecure position of the W.P.A. recreation worker and the carrying through of their work as a matter of routine. The new experience could change the ideology and morale of these people so suddenly and deeply because it provided worth-while goals and a long-range outlook to individuals who previously had lived with a time perspective which was composed of a disagreeable past, unsatisfactory present, and no positive outlook for the future. In other words, the retraining was achieved, not in spite of the long-standing bad habits but, partly, because of them (my bolding) (Lewin 1942, 1997, p226)."

My colleagues and I can bear witness to countless such shifts in even shorter periods of time, as we have applied and refined Lewin's methods. More on that in Chapters 12 and 13.

Lewin summarizes the shift to leading through democratic principles this way: "Learning democracy means, first, that the person has to do something himself instead of being passively moved by forces imposed on him. Second, learning democracy means to establish certain likes and dislikes, that is, certain valences, values, and ideologies. Third, learning democracy means to get acquainted with certain techniques, such as those of group decision (Lewin, 1942, 1997, p223)."

All of which is vital to our next topic, Social Justice and Change, and to the final chapter of Section 2, Organization Development.

Chapter 9
Social Justice and Change

Lewin tackled minority issues, ethnic tensions, and race relations head on. In doing so, of course, he used the language of his times. I ask the reader to bear with the racial designations and the patriarchal language in these original quotes here and elsewhere in the text.

From a strictly scientific perspective the words shouldn't matter (although I recognize that there are connotations with certain words, and hence I wouldn't touch certain words with a ten-foot pole). It can and will be argued here that all racial designations are inaccurate and come from dubious sources. The same holds for sexism in language. Identifying with humanity, and also with ethnic and cultural heritages makes much more sense, and doesn't mean one is denying sexism, racism, and the various holocausts throughout history (the African slave trade, the Jewish holocaust, the Native American genocide, patriarchal oppression of and abuse of women, etc.). I trust Lewin would agree. I have chosen not to take on the awkward task of changing his writing.

Along with the social construction of reality comes the social construction of race. My father has long considered race *Man's Most Dangerous Myth,* as it was put in 1942 by Ashley Montague in a book by that title which dad greatly respects. As dad puts it, "My bottom line is that I resist the idea that there are races. **Race is a social construct.** The idea was invented in Europe in the 15th century to justify colonialism and, therefore, the slave trade. The so-called superior *race* therefore was helping the so-called inferior *races* by enslaving them... Different shades of brown are a result of the journey of we homosapians as we migrated from Africa and populated the planet...those who slowly moved north became light brown (white?). Those who stayed close to the equator remain darker! Certainly, in the American culture people of light brown skin (called *white*) have privileges from birth which most darker skin people do not have! That there are different ethnic groups - yes of course! That in the migration from the Rift Valley in Kenya across the planet different characteristics and skin colors evolved—absolutely!

My National Geographic DNA indicates that I (like everyone else on the planet) came out of Africa 55,000 years ago from Kenya. I am proud that my ancestors lived for 20,000 years in Ethiopia and were possibly members of the Amhara tribe, one of the nine ethnic divisions in that country. I was proud when a Seattle cabdriver from that tribe looked at me and said, 'You look Amhara!' (Crosby, 2019, p240)."

To be clear that he knows race has been and is still used as a basis of discrimination, dad adds, "Some object, even strenuously, to people of my skin color saying, 'There is only one race' as if I am saying, 'Get over it—we're all in the same boat!' *If it is said to whitewash the huge inequalities in our culture, then I don't like the statement either* (Crosby, 2019, p237)." That is why the concept of race is so dangerous—because like gender, and religion, it has been operationalized into "us versus them" beliefs, used by political elites to divide and conquer the people they are ruling, and used by untold millions to justify inequities and the most horrific crimes of the human race. If we are to survive and thrive we must stop such foolishness.

A colleague of mine, Dr. Rodney Coates and his co-authors, Abby Ferber and David Brunsma, have added much needed scientific objectivity to the emotionally charged topic of race.

Cover of *The Matrix of Race*

On page 5 of the preface of their book, Coates et al explain their hypothesis this way:

"The 'matrix' in the title refers to a way of thinking about race that can help readers get beyond the familiar 'us versus them' arguments that can lead to resistance and hostility. This framework incorporates a number of important theories and perspectives from contemporary sociologists who study this subject: (a) Race is socially constructed; it changes from one place to another and across time. (b) When talking about racial inequality, it is more useful to focus on the structures of society (institutions) than to blame individuals. (c) Race is intersectional; it is embedded in other socially constructed categories of difference (like gender, social class, ethnicity, and sexuality). And (d) there are two sides to race: oppression and privilege. Both are harmful, and both can be experienced simultaneously (Coates et al, 2018)."

Let us turn back to Lewin, who was not afraid to apply his own social science to the subject, using the language of the times:

"Definite answers to such questions can be supplied only by an 'experimental cultural anthropology'... (Lewin, 1943, 1997, p35)." Lewin oversaw one such experiment, which indicated that prejudice was a social construct, passed on as most social customs are, from generation to generation:

"Horowitz found no prejudices against Negroes in white children under three years. The prejudices increased between four and six years. This increase was as great in New York as in the South. It was independent of the degree of acquaintance of the children with Negro children, and of the actual status of the Negro child in the class which the white child attended. The prejudices are, however, related to the attitude of the parents of the white child. This indicates that the prejudices against the Negroes are due to an induction and gradual taking-over of the culture of the parents by the child (Lewin, 1946, 1997, p375)."

My grandson does a wonderful job of proving this point of no prejudice thus far. Hopefully the love and modeling in his immediate family will inoculate him against the prejudices in our larger society:

No prejudice (yet!)

Based on his Jewish experience, and his faith in reason, Lewin was able to deeply feel the plight of the minority, without resorting to simply scapegoating the majority. As he put it:

Inter-group relations is a two-way affair. This means that to improve relations between groups both of the interacting groups have to be studied.

In recent years we have started to realize that **so-called minority problems are in fact majority problems,** that the Negro problem is the problem of the white, that the Jewish problem is the problem of the non-Jew, and so on. It is also true of course that inter-group relations cannot be solved without altering certain aspects of conduct and sentiment of the minority group. One of the most severe obstacles in the way of improvement seems to be the notorious lack of confidence and self-esteem of most minority groups. Minority groups tend to accept the implicit judgment of those who have status even where the judgment is directed against themselves... Neither an individual nor a group that is at odds with itself can live normally or live happily with other groups.

It should be clear to the social scientist that it is hopeless to cope with this problem by providing sufficient self-esteem for members of minority groups as individuals. The discrimination which these individuals experience is not directed against them as individuals but as group members and only by raising their self-esteem as group members to the normal level can a remedy be produced...

The solution, I think, can be found only through a development which would bring the general level of group esteem and group loyalty which in themselves are perfectly natural and necessary phenomena to the same level for all groups of society. That means every effort should be made to lower the inflated self-esteem of the 100 percenters. They should learn the prayer from the musical-play, Oklahoma. "Dear God, make me see that I am not better than my fellow men." However it is essential to learn the second half of this prayer that goes something like "but that I am every darn bit as good as he." From the experiences thus far I would judge that raising the self-esteem of the minority groups is one of the most strategic means for the improvement of inter-group relations (my bolding) (Lewin, 1946, 1997, p151).

I love Lewin's clarity that "...so-called minority problems are in fact majority problems." In a story that I also love, and I believe Lewin would have felt the same, my father, in 1962 as a young Methodist minister in Wausau, Wisconsin, echoes Lewin in a speech to the Kiwanis Club at the Hotel Wausau. The white men in the audience were worried that their property values might drop if African Americans were allowed to move into the town (there were no African American residents at the time). As quoted in the local paper, dad told the gathering, "When freedom is denied to anyone, it is denied to me, and to you. There is no freedom for any citizen unless it is for all." He went on to say that when African Americans move into a community property values rise or at least stay the same. Again, like Lewin, using the vernacular of the times, dad told the community, "When people talk about property values, they are talking about our own society and those who discriminate against the Negro."

The paper goes on (this is my favorite part): "The Rev. Mr. Crosby said that the Negro problem is probably not as great as the 'white problem.' We in Wausau need to have a citizens' committee set up to initiate the influx of Negros here," he said, "for if we don't do something to invite them we are really not Christians (*Wausau Daily Herald*, 1962, p1)."

There are more stories of dad walking in Lewin's footsteps in his latest book, *Memoirs of a Change Agent*. As dad and Lewin show, empathy is possible even when one hasn't had the same firsthand experience as another. Empathy with powerlessness is possible for anyone who chooses to recognize it in their own lives. It may come as a surprise to some, but most people have a sense of powerlessness at times even when they are at the top of families, organizations, and political structures, and could tap those experiences to better understand others if they had the awareness and desire to do so. Lewin lived the experience of a powerless minority. He did so with a systemic perspective, always considering behavior within the context of the cultural force field. In his 1941 paper *Self-Hatred Among Jews* he wrote:

Self-hatred seems to be a psychopathological phenomenon, and its prevention may seem mainly a task for the psychiatrist. However, modern psychology knows that many psychological

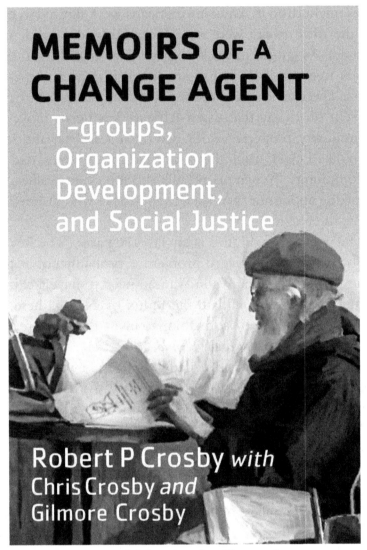

Cover of *Memoirs of a Change Agent*

phenomena are but an expression of a social situation in which the individual finds himself. In a few cases, Jewish self-hatred may grow out of a neurotic or otherwise abnormal personality, but in the great majority of cases it is a phenomenon in persons of normal mental health. In other words, it is a social psychological phenomenon, even though it usually influences deeply the total personality. In fact, neurotic trends in Jews are frequently the result of their lack of adjustment to just such group problems.

Jewish self-hatred will die out only when actual equality of status with the non-Jew is achieved. Only then will the enmity against one's own group decrease to the relatively insignificant proportions characteristic of the majority group's. Sound self-criticism will replace it. This does not mean that nothing can be done meanwhile. After all, we do have a great many Jews who can hardly be classified as anti-Semitic.

The only way to avoid Jewish self-hatred in its various forms is a change of the negative balance between the forces toward and away from the Jewish group into a positive balance, the creation of loyalty to the Jewish group instead of negative chauvinism. We are unable to safeguard our fellow Jews or our growing children today against those handicaps which are the result of their being Jewish. However, we can try to build up a Jewish education both on the children's level and on the adult level to counteract the feeling of inferiority and the feeling of fear which are the most important sources of the negative balance.

The feeling of inferiority of the Jew is but an indication of the fact that he sees things Jewish with the eyes of the unfriendly majority (Lewin, 1941, 1997, p140).

That feeling of fear is important to understand. It shows up not only in the minority experience, but in hierarchical relationships in organizations. Here I turn to another important influence on my father, Howard Thurman. Thurman was dad's pastor during his student days at Boston University, and a mentor to Martin Luther King, Jr. For those of you unfamiliar with Thurman, he wrote the source of the following quotations, *Jesus and the Disinherited,* after traveling to India where he met with Gandhi and others, and grappled with their questioning of whether Christianity was just a means of trapping blacks within systemic oppression in the US. Thurman concluded that under Roman rule Jesus was also "disinherited" by the oppression of the Romans, and that his message speaks directly to how to find dignity through faith and non-violence in the face of oppression.

Writing in 1949 Thurman explains: "Fear is one of the persistent hounds of hell that dog the footsteps of the poor, the dispossessed, the disinherited...The ever-present fear that besets the vast poor, the economically and socially insecure, is a fear of still a different breed. It is a climate closing in; it is like the fog in San Francisco or in London...It has its roots deep in the heart of the relations between the weak and the strong... when the power and the tools of violence are on one side, the fact that there is no available and recognized protection from violence makes the resulting fear deeply terrifying (Thurman, 1949, p36)."

The closest I come to this experience is in my work abroad. I have worked for years in rural Jamaica for example, where I am often the only "white" (pale seems to me more accurate, but I will use the culturally accepted vernacular of my times) person present. The vast majority of Jamaicans have welcomed me with open arms, and the people I work with have become like family. I consider Jamaica my second home. Nonetheless I know that if I am in the wrong place at the wrong time, like the time when the white male mining executive I was with almost ran over a child on a rural road, it is likely that pent up frustrations dating back to slavery will be vented against me. As a temporary minority, I am careful not to get into needless confrontations. On the other hand, unless I did something truly awful the authorities would still likely protect me, so my fear is still mild compared to what Thurman's "dispossessed" must face.

Interestingly, Thurman goes on to address the space of

Cover of *Jesus and the Disinherited*

free movement: "The threat of violence with a well-nigh limitless power is a weapon by which the weak are held in check. Artificial limitations are placed upon them, restricting freedom of movement, of employment, and of participation in the common life. These limitations are given formal or informal expression in general or specific policies of separateness and segregation (Thurman, 1949, p41)."

As a child I lived in formal segregation in the early 1960s in Nashville, Tennessee. When my parents had African American friends over, we received death threats over the phone (which I and my siblings were blissfully unaware of). Mom would give them a piece of her mind and hang up.

I recognize now that I grew up in a very different experience of America than African American children of the same age. I grew up believing the good guys were on my side, like "Officer Friendly" and the US GIs that won WWII. Little did I know that the black community lived in fear of the same authorities, as they still do today during what should be routine traffic stops. I'm afraid of a ticket, they're afraid of being choked to death or shot[1]. And the confidence to turn to the police for help is just one example of the many privileges I have received, which I was oblivious to for much of my life. Privileges gained simply due to being born a male in my ethnic group in a racist and sexist society. I still wonder now whether I would have gotten my first job had I been African American, etc. etc.

Like Lewin, Thurman notes that prejudice poisons the oppressor and the oppressed, and he also was mindful of the similarities between the African American and the Jewish experience, along with that of other minorities: "The fear that segregation inspires among the weak in turn breeds fear among the strong and the dominant. This fear insulates the conscience against a sense of wrongdoing in carrying out a policy of segregation. For it counsels that if there were no segregation, there would be no protection against invasion of the home, the church, the school...The Jewish community has long been acquainted with segregation and the persecution growing out of it (Thurman, 1949, p44)."

In an environment of past and present oppression, there

---

1 This was written before the video of George Floyd's murder and the subsequent protests. I am gaurdedly hopeful for real progress as I do these final edits on Juneteenth 2020.

is high-intensity fear and there is low-intensity fear. There are big overt aggressions, such as a police action, and countless small covert aggressions. The latter have recently been labeled "micro-aggressions" or "micro-invalidations." The cumulative effect of real or perceived micro-aggressions can put a person on high alert for life, damage their self-esteem, and make them a nervous wreck. Some micro-aggressions are intentional, as when my dad was told that his best friend in high school, an African American, couldn't be served at dad's favorite restaurant (at 91, dad is still upset about it). Others are not intentional as when my wife, a dark-skinned (as she prefers to put it) Jamaican, had a Hispanic co-worker tell her, "To me you're not black. You're white." The co-worker seemed oblivious of the inherent racism in her intended compliment.

Long before the term was coined, Lewin spoke of the effect of micro-aggressions and of the understandable difficulty facing the minority individual as they tried to distinguish between what is real discrimination and what is imagined:

"*Unclearness* as to whether, in a given case, a set-back is due to the individual's lack of ability or due to anti-Semitism. If the young Jew is refused a job, is not invited to a birthday party, is not asked to join a club, he is usually not fully clear as to whether he himself is to blame or whether he is being discriminated against. A person who knows that his own shortcomings have caused his failure may do something to overcome them, or, if that is not possible, he can decide to apply his efforts in other directions.

If he knows that his being refused has nothing to do with his own abilities he will not blame himself, and instead may try to change the social reality. However, if he is in doubt as to whether his own shortcomings are the cause of his experience, he will be disorientated. He will intermittently blame himself and refuse responsibility, blame the others and be apologetic. In other words, this unclearness necessarily leads to a disorganized emotional behavior on the area of self-esteem which is so important for adjustment and personality development (Lewin, 1941, 1999, p329)."

The issue of real or perceived slights is confusing for the majority and the minority, and is a further restraining force in overcoming prejudice. As long as there is sexism, the same unclearness will infect gender relationships as well. For those who have been in a group that has suffered discrimination, it's understandable to suspect racism, sexism, or any other "ism" in any unsatisfactory interactions. My wife wondered about it in many interactions when she first migrated to the US; less so as time has gone by. I have seen this (with other individuals besides my wife) go to the extreme of adamantly believing it is there even when I had strong reason to believe it wasn't. On the flip side, for those from a group that have been in power, it is easy to defensively deny the validity of any such fears, and to be blind to such dynamics even when they are genuinely happening.

The confusion in US society about these dynamics reared its head in an experience two of my colleagues, both white males, had recently. They were teaching *The Interpersonal Gap* model (Appendix A) of interpersonal communications in a T-group based workshop. The simple version of the model is that if there is a difference between the intent of the sender and the impact on the receiver, that is a gap, which is inherently a misunderstanding. A young African American woman took offense to the model and claimed that if a person (the receiver ...her in this case) felt harmed by something someone else (the sender) did or said it was 100% the responsibility of the sender and they should apologize. When my colleagues stuck with their belief that how one receives messages is also important, and that it is easy to misunderstand on the receiving end, they were confronted as racist based on the young woman's understanding of the "micro-aggression" training she had recently received.

In personal correspondence about this incident, Dr. Rodney Coates (the aforementioned author of *The Matrix of Race*) had this to say: "One word—well 2—bs... that's called playing the race card...and makes any kind of real work and progress impossible. Look...whites are not guilty by virtue of being white; neither are blacks victims by virtue of being black. The problem with the victim shame blame game is that we don't get anywhere. That's why I favor restorative and not retributive justice.

Let me clarify if I can. A couple years ago I'm in my office talking to a black student, and a colleague passed by, saw me in the office, and said 'boy, did you see that.' The student looking aghast said 'He just called you boy.' I said, 'No its an expression...' We filter things through layers of experiences, trauma, stress, pain and joy. And often times when there is no trust we misread what is being said. It means we must listen even more carefully...we must extend trust that bridges across the valleys of distrust.

(That is) why micro-aggression and blind spots are the wrong way to start conversations about diversity. For if there are these deep-seated hostilities, biases, micro-aggression and blind spots then there should also be a corollary set of deep seated, fundamental values of good will that extends to all, regardless of identities. Conversations that begin and end with the former, and not the latter...only tell one side of the story (Coates, 2018)."

The path forward to end prejudice and discrimination... to end all intolerance...must be walked together. As Lewin put it, the only intolerance must be "the intolerance of the intolerant."

True to form, Lewin was clear that an age where everyone is granted equal rights and perceived with equal respect won't come by minority individuals pulling themselves up by their bootstraps one person at a time into the majority culture, even though "fitting in" has long been an understandable and crazy-making aspiration of the oppressed. Inequality and prejudice are systemic issues and require systemic answers:

It is well to realize that every underprivileged minority group is kept together not only by cohesive forces among its members but also by the boundary which the majority erects against the crossing of an individual from the minority to the majority group. It is in the interest of the majority to keep the minority in its underprivileged status. There are minorities which are kept together almost entirely by such a wall around them. The members of these minorities show certain typical characteristics resulting from this situation. Every individual likes to gain in social status. Therefore the member of an underprivileged group will try to leave it for the more privileged majority. In other words, he will try to do what in the case of Negroes is called 'passing,' in the case of Jews, 'assimilation.' It would be an easy solution of the minority problem if it could be done away with through individual assimilation. Actually, however, such a solution is impossible for any underprivileged group. Equal rights for women could not be attained by one after the other being granted the right to vote; the Negro problem cannot be solved by individual 'passing.' A few Jews might be fully accepted by non-Jews. This chance, however, is today more meager than ever and certainly it is absurd to believe that fifteen million Jews can sneak over the boundary one by one.

What then is the situation of a member of a minority group kept together merely by the repulsion of the majority? The basic factor in his life is his wish to cross this insuperable boundary. Therefore, he lives almost perpetually in a state of conflict and tension. He dislikes or even hates his own group because it is nothing but a burden to him. Like an adolescent who does not wish to be a child any longer but who knows that he is not accepted as an adult, such a person stands at the borderline of his group, being neither here nor there. He is unhappy and shows the typical characteristics of a marginal man who does not know where he belongs. A Jew of this type will dislike everything specifically Jewish, for he will see in it that which keeps him away from the majority for which he is longing. He will show dislike for those Jews who are outspokenly so and will frequently indulge in self-hatred.

There is one more characteristic peculiar to minority groups kept together merely by outside pressure as contrasted with the members of a minority who have a positive attitude towards their own group. The latter group will have an organic life of its own. It will show organization and inner strength. A minority kept together only from outside is in itself chaotic. It is composed of a mass of individuals without inner relations with each other, a group unorganized and weak (Lewin, 1939, 1997, p119)."

The following topographical drawing (Figure 9.1) depicts the minority person on the margin between the majority group and their own group.

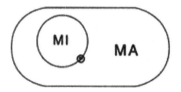

The marginal man. The person (*P*) stand-
ing on the boundary between the minority group *MI* and the
majority group *MA*.

Figure 9.1
The marginal man (Lewin, 1940, 1997, p130)

Going where no one had gone before, Lewin set out to

do action research to better understand discrimination and prejudice, and to eradicate it. From the time that he launched the Commission for Community Interrelations (C.C.I.) until the time of his death, Lewin and his staff "handled more than fifty separate different projects involving all four varieties of action research (Marrow, 1969, p203)." The following are a few examples, documented by Marrow and elsewhere.

In one of his bolder studies, Lewin pondered the effects of segregation versus integration in public housing, and how to effectively bring ethnic groups together. Inter-racial housing was a new concept in post-war America. Lewin's study offered two types of occupancy, segregated housing in a checkerboard pattern, or integrated buildings "filled on a first come first serve basis, without regard of color...

The results disclosed a sharp contrast in attitudes... in the segregated projects resentments towards Negroes were much sharper and anti-negro prejudice stronger; indeed the white residents expressed strong preference for even greater segregation.

On the other hand, where whites came to know Negroes as next door neighbors, they shared a growing sense of common humanity which relaxed the tensions they had brought with them and replaced antagonism with friendliness. The change was expressed (among other responses) by their preference for more and more integrated housing.

Group cohesiveness and morale were higher in the integrated than in the segregated projects. White residents in integrated housing, despite initial forebodings, came to like living in them and many of them expressed pride in their building's 'democracy' (Marrow, 1969, p209)."

Lewin's work demonstrated that separation is a restraining force holding fear and prejudice in place. This is true for race relations as well as for industrial relations.

C.C.I. helped the community of Coney Island address gang

behavior by building a successful relationship between a C.C.I. staff member and the gang (which began in exchange for waiving legal charges after an attack on Jewish youth), but also by "providing more and better housing, building recreational centers... improving transportation (Marrow, 1969, p204)." The study achieved three of its goals. The gang "learned to behave in a way more acceptable to the community" (which meant less fighting amongst other criteria). The gang's energies were "redirected towards more constructive activities." Less progress was made in terms of changing their prejudices. Based in the C.C.I research, "the changes endured after the consultant was withdrawn (Marrow, 1968, p204)."

Another project took the form of legal action to combat discrimination. "Conferring with Lewin ..." the American Jewish Congress, the funding body for the C.C.I., sued the Medical School of Columbia University over their "quota for Jews." Columbia denied any such quota system, and refused to turn over their selection system records, but they settled out of court, agreed to establish a transparent system, stated publicly that "applicants would be judged without regard for race or religion," and the victory "...resulted in a revision of discriminatory policies by leading schools of higher learning throughout the country (Marrow, 1969, p206)."

In another study, department stores were unwilling to hire African Americans as sales clerks because, "...as the store management put it, our customers wouldn't stand for it." C.C.I.'s research concluded that a large percentage of shoppers who admitted to racial prejudice in a survey kept shopping at their preferred store even when they were waited on by African Americans. The study concluded that the "...fear that sales would be hurt was not supported by the evidence (Marrow, 1969, p206)."

Finally, we come to perhaps the greatest action research project ever (to date), both for its goals, to decrease racial tensions in the State of Connecticut, but also for its surprise outcome: the invention of a learning method based on group dynamics that gets straight to the heart of re-education of the social construction of reality—the T-group. The next chapter is devoted to that "marvelous moment," as my father puts it.

Chapter 10
The Birth of the T-group

At the Connecticut workshop (from left to right): Frank Wright (possibly Dr. Frank Simpson[1]), Leah Gold Fine, Kurt Lewin, Leland Bradford and Ken Benne

As Lewin tells the story:

One example may illustrate the potentialities of co-operation between practitioners and social scientists. In the beginning of this year the Chairman of the Advisory Committee on Race Relations for the State of Connecticut, who is at the same time a leading member of the Interracial <u>Commission of</u> the State of Connecticut, approached us with

1 Whover wrote the caption in Marrow's book mistakenly mixed up Benne and Bradford (corrected above). Dr. Frank Simpson was the commission member who solicited Lewin's services and I suspect a second mistake was misnaming him "Wright."

a request to conduct a workshop for fifty community workers in the field of intergroup relations from all over the state of Connecticut.

A project emerged in which three agencies co-operated, the Advisory Committee on Intergroup Relations of the State of Connecticut, The Commission on Community Interrelations of the American Jewish Congress, and the Research Center for Group Dynamics at the Massachusetts Institute of Technology. The State Advisory Committee is composed of members of the Interracial Commission of the State of Connecticut, a member of the State Department of Education of the State of Connecticut, and the person in charge of the Connecticut Valley Region of the Conference of Christians and Jews. The state of Connecticut seems to be unique in having an interracial commission as a part of its regular government. It was apparent that any improvement of techniques which could be linked with this strategic central body would have a much better chance of a wide-spread and lasting effect. After a thorough discussion of various possibilities the following change-experiment was designed co-operatively.

Recent research findings have indicated that the ideologies and stereotypes which govern inter-group relations should not be viewed as individual character traits but that they are anchored in cultural standards, that their stability and their change depend largely on happenings in groups as groups. Experience with leadership training had convinced us that the workshop setting is among the most powerful tools for bringing about improvement of skill in handling inter-group relations.

Even a good and successful workshop, however, seems seldom to have the chance to lead to long-range improvements in the field of inter-group relations. The individual who comes home from the workshop full of enthusiasm and new insights will again have to face the community, one against perhaps

100,000. Obviously, the chances are high that his success will not be up to his new level of aspiration, and that soon disappointments will set him back again. We are facing here a question which is of prime importance for any social change, namely the problem of its permanence.

To test certain hypotheses in regard to the effect of individual as against group settings, the following variations were introduced into the experimental workshop. Part of the delegates came as usual, one individual from a town. For a number of communities, however, it was decided the attempt would be made to secure a number of delegates and if possible to develop in the workshop teams who would keep up their team relationship after the workshop. This should give a greater chance for permanency of the enthusiasm and group productivity and should also multiply the power of the participants to bring about the desired change. A third group of delegates to the workshop would receive a certain amount of expert help even after they returned to the community...

The methods of recording the essential events of the workshop included an evaluation session at the end of every day. Observers who had attended the various subgroup sessions reported (into a recording machine) the leadership pattern they had observed, the progress or lack of progress in the development of the groups from a conglomeration of individuals to an integrated "we" and so on (Lewin, 1941, 1997, p148).

Several elements of what became the T-group (the T stood for training) were woven into the Connecticut experiment from the beginning:

1. The training would take place in the form of a workshop, in this case lasting two weeks, away from the regular work environment of the participants.

2. In Connecticut there were three working groups - a skilled

facilitator led each group (Ron Lippitt, Leland Bradford, and Ken Benne).

3. The participants were taught communication, conflict management, and other applicable skills. Planned "re-education" of the "social construction of reality" took place through brief lectures on social science theory, interaction with and influence by the faculty, interaction with the other workshop participants (a highly diverse group), and immersion in the democratic principles of the process.

4. Behavioral observation was a carefully crafted part of the process.

5. Teams were included so as to leverage group dynamics in sustaining the learning after the workshop.

My father, who experienced his first T-group in 1953, maintained all five of these elements in his adaptation of T-group methodology. I will recap these in Chapter 12 along with other elements which emerged during the workshop.

The idea of taking the participants out of their normal working environment became a valuable OD option:

"Sometimes the value system of this face-to-face group conflicts with the values of the larger cultural setting and it is necessary to separate the group from the larger setting. For instance, during retraining of recreational leaders from autocratic to democratic patterns Bavelas was careful to safeguard them from interference by the administration of the recreational center. The effectiveness of camps or workshops in changing ideology or conduct depends in part on the possibility of creating such 'cultural islands' during change. The stronger the accepted subculture of the workshop and the more isolated it is the more will it minimize that type of resistance to change which is based on the relation between the individual and the standards of the larger group (Lewin,

1947, 1997, p332)."

The observers played a vital role and were young graduate students in social psychology connected in one way or the other to Lewin and has staff. One, Melvin "Mef" Seeman (1918–2020), was still alive at 101 years of age and of reasonably sound mind at the time of this writing. He enthusiastically spoke with me several times, sharing his warm feelings about Lewin and the workshop although his memory of the details had understandably faded. Sadly, Mr. Seeman passed away Janauary 31st, 2020. RIP Mef.

As mentioned, Mef and the other researchers silently took behavioral notes during the day, and then reviewed them with the faculty in the evening. An observer might report: "At 10AM Mrs. X attacked the group leader. Mr. Y came to the defense of the leader and he and Mrs. X became involved in a heated exchange. Some other members were drawn into taking sides. Other members seemed frightened and tried to make peace. But they were ignored by the combatants. At 10:10AM the leader came back in to redirect attention to the problem… (Bradford et al, 1964, p82)." They also kept careful stats on both the faculty and the participants with strictly behavioral data such as who spoke, how many times, and to whom. Part of the intention was to derive lessons learned from the behavior of the three leaders.

Some of the participants commuted home in the evenings, while the majority stayed at the workshop location, on the Teachers College campus in New Britain, Connecticut. Early in the workshop, three of the participants caught wind of the evening faculty session, and inquired as to whether they could listen in. There are various versions of what happened next. It seems likely that some of the staff were initially stressed by the intrusion and inclined to keep the session private. Marrow reports that, "Most of the staff feared it would be harmful to have the trainees sit in while their behavior was being discussed (Marrow, 1969, p212)." Whatever the case in every version, Lewin, true to form, clearly and warmly welcomed the participants in. According to Warren Bennis, as they sat quietly listening, "They were fascinated by what they heard. Analyzing how a group formed and evolved was much more fun than simply being in one (Bennis, 2010)."

According to Ron Lippitt, "Sometime during the evening an observer made some remarks about the behavior of one of the three persons that were sitting in—a woman trainee. She broke in to disagree with the observation and described it from her point of view. For a while there was quite an active dialogue between the research observer, the trainer, and the trainee about the interpretation of the event, with Kurt an active prober, obviously enjoying this different source of data that had to be coped with and integrated.

At the end of the evening the trainees asked if they could come back for the next meeting at which their behavior would be evaluated. Kurt, feeling that it had been a valuable contribution rather than an intrusion, enthusiastically agreed to their return. The next night at least half of the fifty or sixty participants were there as the result of the grapevine reporting of the activity by the three participants.

The evening session from then on became the significant learning experience of the day, with the focus on actual behavioral events and with active dialogue about differences of interpretation and observations of the events by those who had participated in them.

The staff were equally enthusiastic, for they found the process a unique way of securing data and interpreting behavior. In addition the staff discovered that feedback had the effect of making participants more sensitive to their own conduct and brought criticism into the open in a healthy and constructive way (Marrow, 1969)."

A participant that attended the next evening's debrief

wrote this in their journal: "I think the thing that impressed me the most was how eager Dr. Benne and the other faculty leaders seemed to be to enter into critical analysis of their own leadership, and to make changes in their plans and performance if better ideas seemed to be forthcoming. This attitude seemed to make it possible for all of us to enter into this type of objective and constructive discussion (Lippitt, 1949, p140)."

By the next evening Lewin had expanded the invitation to all of the workshop participants. Each evening more and more came. Often, upon hearing the review, they became dynamically engaged and sometimes defensive about the information. "Lewin and the others realized that a group that scrutinized its own process as it formed and changed was something new and valuable (Bennis, 2010)."

My father's associate (and my colleague) Dr. John Scherer was also mentored by Lippitt. Dad quotes John's recollection of a conversation between the three of them thusly, "John Scherer writes, 'Ron Lippitt told Bob and me it was like an electric current went through Lewin as he got excited about what was happening *in that moment*—the difference being surfaced between the way the two participants had experienced *what happened* and what his faculty had experienced...(Crosby, 2019)." As Bradford put it, the result was like a "tremendous electric charge...as people reacted to data about their own behavior (Marrow, 1969, p212)."

Dad continues, "According to Bradford, Gibb, Benne, in 1964, 'To the training staff it seemed that a potentially powerful medium and process of re-education was somewhat inadvertently hit upon.' During a group conversation they decided that the following year they would report these interaction dynamics in the midst of the discussions! Most participants are unaware of such dynamics except at some level of discomfort when tension surfaces. In this way participants would learn how to focus on the processes that are constantly taking place between them and the other people in the conversation as well as the content. Thus was birthed the T-group which still creates an electric moment of openness for most new participants (Crosby, 2019)."

A new clarity about action research also began to emerge during this historic event. In Lewin's summary of the workshop he elevates the role of training in his methodology. Indeed, Lippitt calls it "training-action-research" in his 1949 book *Training in Community Relations*, which is completely dedicated to the planning, execution, and evaluation of the Connecticut workshop. Here is what Lewin had to say:

I have been deeply impressed with the tremendous pedagogical effect which these evaluation meetings, designed for the purpose of scientific recording, had on the training process. The atmosphere of objectivity, the readiness by the faculty to discuss openly their mistakes, far from endangering their position, seemed to lead to an enhancement of appreciation and to bring about that mood of relaxed objectivity which is nowhere more difficult to achieve than in the field of inter-group relations which is loaded with emotionality and attitude rigidity even among the so-called liberals and those whose job it is to promote inter-group relations.

This and similar experiences have convinced me that **we should consider action, research, and training as a triangle** that should be kept together for the sake of any of its corners (Figure 10.1, next page). It is seldom possible to improve the action pattern without training personnel. In fact today the lack of competent training personnel is one of the greatest hindrances to progress in setting up more experimentation. The training of large numbers of social scientists who can handle scientific problems but are also equipped for the delicate task of building productive, hard-hitting teams with practitioners is a prerequisite for progress in social science as well as in social management for intergroup relations.

As I watched, during the workshop, the delegates from different towns all over Connecticut transform from a multitude of unrelated individuals, frequently opposed in their outlook and their interests, into co-operative teams not on the basis of sweetness but on the basis of readiness to face difficulties realistically, to apply honest fact-finding, and to work together to overcome them; when I saw the pattern of role-playing emerge, saw the major responsibilities move slowly according to plan from the faculty to the trainees; when I saw, in the final session, the State Advisory Committee receive the backing of the delegates for a plan of linking the teachers colleges throughout the state with certain aspects of group relations within the communities; when I heard the delegates and teams of delegates from various towns present their plans for city workshops and a number of other projects to go into realization immediately, I could not help feeling that the close integration of action, training, and research holds tremendous possibilities for the field of inter-group relations. I would like to pass on this feeling to you (my bolding) (Lewin, 1946, 1997, p149)."

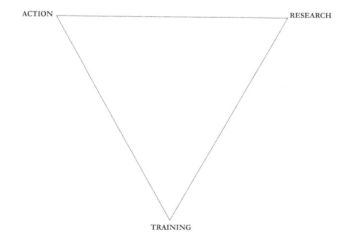

Figure 10.1

Training, action, and research as a triangle (Crosby, 2020)

Besides the birth of the T-group, which we will return to in Chapter 12, the Connecticut workshop was successful on many levels, including the all-important goal of transferring the methods of the social scientist to the community so that they could continue with their own action research activities. As Marrow put it, "Lewin believed that **the social scientists may serve principally as consultants or guides, so that the inquiry can be carried on with a high degree of technical competence. But the work must be done by the citizens themselves. Any group of people must cure itself of its sickness on the basis of its own diagnosis and treatment** (my bolding) (Marrow, 1969, p221)."

Based on the situation, substitute the word "employees" for the word "citizens" in the sentence above. True to his quest for a universal theory, Lewin applied the same methods in industrial settings. Let us turn our attention there now.

Chapter 11
Organization Development

While acknowledged by most sources as the founder of organization development, there is no evidence Lewin ever used the term. Instead, according to "...Lippitt, the name was coined independently but simultaneously by two groups of NTL consultants: Robert Blake and Herbert Shepard working at Esso and Richard Beckhard and Douglas McGregor working at General Mills. It is also clear that most of those who became leading figures in the OD movement were involved in the NTL and shared its zealot-like commitment to the promotion of T-groups, which created the conditions for the rapid expansion of OD in the 1960s (Burnes and Cooke, 2012, p1400)."

Bernard Burnes tells this version (in another article – one of several articles he has written or co-authored about Lewin) of Lewin's first foray into applying his social science and planned change methods within industry:

"Marrow met Lewin in 1934 when he consulted Lewin about his PhD topic. By 1937, when Marrow received his doctorate, they were firm friends. Marrow was torn between a career in the family business or in academia. Lewin convinced him he could do both, pointing out that Marrow's role at Harwood would allow him a unique position to conduct research. As A. J. Marrow...commented, 'I decided to follow Lewin's advice. I realized that with the power of chief executive, I could set up research programs that would provide insights into the management of people in organizations and thereby discover new ways to get people to attain their potential and work at their best (Burnes, 2019, p401)."

It was a mutually beneficial relationship. Marrow became a believer in Lewin and his methods. He continued applying them long after Lewin's death. Lewin's action research at Harwood sharpened his clarity about group dynamics. For example, according to Marrow, Lewin's experiments at Harwood showed that "...if a group sets the range or level of productivity in a factory, any attempt on the part of any single employee to deviate from that standard heightens the normal social pressure of his co-workers to push him back into line. The further he deviates from the norm, the stronger the pressure on him to conform to it.

When Lewin studied this problem at the Harwood plant in 1940, he concluded that it is futile to try to change any worker from one pattern to another unless the entire group to which he 'belongs' is included in the change (Marrow, 1969, p169)."

Lewin's work at Harwood led to measurable and sustainable productivity improvements. As Burns puts it:

"Though the collaboration between Harwood and Lewin ended with his untimely death in 1947, it did not end Harwood's commitment to his participative approach to managing and changing organizations. This had brought significant benefits to the company: sales had increased by 300%, productivity by 20%, there was a 50% reduction in quality problems, a 45% reduction in absenteeism, a 65% reduction in labor turnover, and worker participation in decision making was the norm (*Human Relations Raises Sales 300%*, 1948). In A. J. Marrow's (1969, p145) words, Lewin's "experimentation at Harwood had a very positive effect on 'practical factory needs'..."

John French left after Lewin's death, but he was replaced as plant psychologist by Dr. Gilbert David. His remit was to continue developing participative management. For example, David conducted an experiment aimed at reducing labor turnover and absenteeism among new recruits in their first 13 weeks of employment. The result was that turnover was 6% among the experimental group, but remained around 55% for the control group, and the corresponding figures for absenteeism were 3% and 10% (Burnes, 2019, p402)."

Bringing force field analysis to bear, Lewin, in *The Special Case of Germany*, writes the following about culture change: "To be stable a cultural change has to penetrate more or less into all aspects of a nation's life. The change in short has to be a change in the 'cultural atmosphere,' not merely a change in single items (Lewin, 1943, 1997, p42)." In the same passage, Lewin elaborates:

General Aspects of Culture Change

Culture as an equilibrium. A culture is not a painted picture—it is a living process, composed of countless social interactions. Like a river whose form and velocity are determined by the balance of those forces that tend to make the water flow faster, and the friction that tends to make the water flow more slowly —the cultural pattern of a people at a given time is maintained by a balance of counteracting forces. The study of cultures on a smaller scale indicates that, for instance, the speed of production or other aspects of a factory has to be understood as an equilibrium, or more precisely, as an 'equilibrium in movement.'

Once a given level is established, certain self-regulatory processes come into function which tend to keep the group life on that level. One speaks of "work habits," "established customs," the "accepted way of doing things." Special occasions may bring about a momentary rise of production, a festival may create for a day or two a different social atmosphere between management and workers, but quickly the effect of the "shot in the arm" will fade out and the basic constellation of forces will re-establish the old forms of everyday living.

The general problem, therefore, of changing the social atmosphere of a factory or of German culture can be formulated somewhat more precisely in this way: How can a situation be brought about which would permanently change the level on which the counteracting forces find their quasi-stationary equilibrium?

1. *Changing the constellation of forces*

To bring about any change, the balance between the forces which maintain the social self-regulation at a given level has to be upset.

2. *Establishing a new cultural pattern*

Hand in hand with the destruction of the forces maintaining the old equilibrium must go the establishment (or liberation) of forces toward a new equilibrium. Not only is it essential to create the fluidity necessary for change and to effect the change itself; it is also imperative that steps be taken to bring about the permanence of the new situation through self-regulation on the new level (Lewin, 1943, 1997, p42).

Self-regulation on the new level comes from shifting the group dynamics from a restraining force to a driving force through the skillful application of training combined with the democratic process of action research. To do so likewise requires changing the power structure from a restraining force to a driving force for the new culture:

"**One point should be seen clearly and strongly. There is no individual who does not, consciously or unconsciously, try to influence his family, his group friends, his occupational group, and so on.** Management is, after all, a legitimate and one of the most important functions in every aspect of social life. **Few aspects are as much befogged in the minds of many as the problems of leadership and of power in a democracy...We have to realize that power itself is an essential aspect of any and every group...**Not the least service which social research can do for society is to attain better insight into the legitimate and non-legitimate aspects of power (my bolding) (Marrow, 1969, p172)."

From Lewin's perspective, culture change that does not include the top of a hierarchy or that skips layers is unlikely to have a lasting effect:

"The experiments in training of democratic leaders, for instance, of foremen in a factory indicate strongly that it does not suffice to have the subleaders who deal with the small face-to-face groups trained in democratic procedures, **if the power above them, such as the management of the factory, does not understand and does not apply democratic procedures...the effect of democratic leadership in the lower brackets will quickly fade** (my bolding) (Lewin, 1943, 1997, p38)." As my father puts it, "Managers/supervisors will manage, *not as they are told to manage at a training, but as they are managed* (Crosby, 2019, p117)!"

In *The Dynamics of Group Action* (Lewin, 1944, 1999, p289) Lewin underscores the importance of leadership development to planned and sustained change:

Democratic Leadership

In all of the experiments mentioned, the problem of leadership plays an important role. As the earlier experiments show...**a group atmosphere can be changed radically in a relatively short time by introducing new leadership techniques...**

Autocratic and democratic leadership consists of playing a certain role. These roles of the leader cannot be carried through without the followers playing certain complementary roles, namely, those of an autocratic or a democratic follower. Educating a group of people in democracy or re-educating them from either autocracy or laissez-faire cannot be accomplished by a passive behavior of the democratic leader. It is a fallacy to assume that individuals, if left alone, will form themselves naturally into democratic groups—it is much more likely that chaos or a primitive pattern of organization through autocratic dominance will result. Establishing democracy in a group implies an active education. **The democratic follower has to learn to play a role which implies, among other points, a fair share of responsibility toward the group and a sensitivity to other people's feelings.** Sometimes, particularly in the beginning of the process of re-education, individuals may have to be made aware in a rather forceful manner of the two-way interdependence which exists between themselves and others within a democratic group. **To create such a change the leader has to be in power and has to be able to hold his power.** As the followers learn democracy, other aspects of the democratic leader's power and function become prevalent.

What holds for the education of democratic followers holds true also for the education of democratic leaders. In fact, it seems to be the same process through which persons learn to play either of these roles, and it seems that both roles have to be learned if either one is to be played well.

1. It is important to realize that democratic behavior cannot be learned by autocratic means. **This does not mean that democratic education or democratic leadership has to diminish the power aspect of group organization in a way which would place the group life on the laissez-faire point of the triangle.** Efficient democracy means organization, but it means organization and leadership on different principles than autocracy.

These principles might be clarified by lectures, but they can be learned, finally, only by democratic living. The 'training on the job' of the democratic leaders...is but one example for the fact that teaching democracy presupposes the establishing of a democratic atmosphere (my bolding).

In Lewinian planned change, people in positions of power must be engaged in the change, whether within organizations such as Harwood, or in community change such as in Connecticut (where business leaders and newspaper editors were invited into the process). To do so, individuals in positions of power need "on the job training" in effective leading and following. The restraining force is not hierarchy. The restraining force in most systems is lack of clarity about effective authority through democratic principles, and an over-abundance of autocratic or laissez-faire leadership (and followership). *Power is part of the system, and must be part of the change or it will surely become a restraining force.*

White and Lippitt conclude that, "The most efficient procedure does appear to be, as a rule, democracy—if democracy is sharply differentiated from laissez-faire, with clear acceptance not only of active leadership but also of the firm use of authority when firmness is called for, and explicit delegation of authority to certain individuals when such delegation is appropriate. A leader or boss must be prepared at one time to exert authority so broadly and energetically that his opponents are sure to call him *autocratic*, and at other times to let other people take all the initiative...or all the glory. A parent, teacher, or employer who wants to be *democratic* and also efficient should continually seek to broaden the base of participation in decision making, whenever participation is really functional and not too time consuming; yet they should usually (not always) exert active leadership and they should unhesitatingly, without the slightest feeling of guilt, use their natural authority whenever the situation calls for firm control or for swift, decisive coordinated action (White and Lippitt, 1960, p292)."

With leadership comes the force field created by goal clarity (or the lack of it). Goal clarity is a key driving or restraining force. On the extreme end of clarity, Lewin witnessed the effect of a true "burning platform" in the midst of his work at Harwood:

"This chapter was written before December 7, 1941; now we are at war. The effect on the morale of the country has been immediate and striking—a circumstance which bears out some of the points we have discussed...

Before December 7, what was a realistic outlook for one individual was doubted by a second and ridiculed as impossible by a third. Now the situation has been clarified. Countless conflicts, whether among factions in the population or within each individual himself, have ceased now that the major aspects of the time perspectives are definitely set.

Being within this new and definite situation means that certain basic goals and necessary actions are "given." In such a situation no special effort is required to keep morale high. The very combination of a definite objective, the belief in final success, and the realistic facing of great difficulties is high morale. The individual who makes extreme efforts and accepts great risks for worth-while goals does not feel that he is making a sacrifice instead, he merely feels that he is acting naturally (Lewin, 1942, 1997, p92)."

Of course, not all goals are as clear and inspiring as defending a nation from attack and defeating totalitarianism, nor do they need to be. Over-hyping the current needs of an organization creates a counterforce of skepticism and mistrust. Like Chicken Little, when the organization truly needs extraordinary focus and effort, credibility may be hard to achieve. On the other hand, a lack of sensible yet challenging goals is like a petri dish for the restraining forces of lethargy, lack of focus, and low morale. During times of relative stability *and* during times of challenge goals must be consistently set that are *both challenging and achievable* if goal clarity is to be leveraged as a driving force for higher productivity and morale.

"One aspect of time perspective which is essential for morale is realism. Here again we encounter the same paradox as that underlying productivity: one criterion of morale is the height of the goal level which the individual is ready to accept seriously. **For high morale, the objective to be reached will represent a great step forward from the present state of affairs...Morale demands both a goal sufficiently above the present state of affairs, and an effort to reach the distant goal through actions planned with sufficient realism to promise an actual step forward.** One might say that this paradox—to be realistic, and at the same time be guided by high goals—lies at the heart of the problem of morale, at least as far as time perspective is concerned (my bolding) (Lewin, 1942, 1997, p90)."

This brings us back to *the application of democratic principles* and the aforementioned *group decision as a change procedure.* Under Lewin's guidance, groups at Harwood influenced their own production rates. This did not occur in a vacuum of course. If the groups had set too low a rate, management have to intervene. Group members understand these dynamics, and are much more likely to stretch themselves than to advocate for a low level of performance.

On a related note, while reflecting on Harwood, Lewin notes that *discussion without decision does not have nearly the impact on productivity and morale as discussion and decision*:

"...it is one thing to be motivated, another to transform motivation into concrete goals and into stabilizing these goals in a way which would carry the individual through to the actual completion of the work. Controlled experiments under comparable conditions show that a discussion without decision did not lead to a parallel increase in production. There are indications that, even if the discussion leads to the general decision of raising production without setting definite production goals to be reached in a definite time, the effect is much less marked (Lewin, 1944, 1999, p288)."

Lewin's action research clearly supported the effectiveness of group decision, as described in the following excerpt from *The Dynamics of Group Action* (Lewin, 1944, 1999, p287):

Discussion, Decision, and Action

In school as well as in industry, certain standards exist concerning the rate of learning or production. These standards are set up by the teacher or the management and are upheld by these authorities with a certain amount of pressure. It is assumed that relaxing the standards will slow down the work of the group members.

This assumption is probably true, but it has little to do with the problem of democracy. Lowering the standards or relaxing the pressure to keep up the standards in an autocratic atmosphere means shifting to a softer form of autocracy... It does not mean a shift in the direction of democracy. **Such a shift would involve...a shift from imposed goals to goals which the group has set for itself.**

It is by no means certain that production goals set for themselves by work teams...would be higher than those ordered by an authority. However, it is by no means certain that they would be lower...

Experiments in industry under controlled conditions show a substantial permanent increase of production created in a short time by certain methods of 'team decision,' an increase in production that was not accomplished by many months of the usual factory pressure (my bolding).

The following graphic (Figure 11.1) supports the power of group decision making:

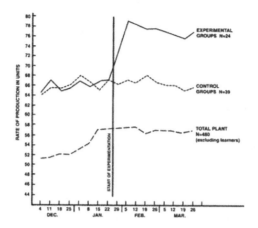

Effect of group decision and pacing cards in a sewing factory.

Figure 11.1
Effect of group decision...(Lewin, 1947, 1997, p320)

It is hard to imagine an approach to planned change that embodies more respect for the individual than Lewin's methods. Leaders are not to be vilified...they are to be taught democratic principles. Workers, citizens, and students are to be engaged in dialogue and decision making. Lewin's empathy and democratic values shone through in everything he did, inside and outside of industry. It is good fortune that the same values, applied with effective methodology, consistently lead to the best results.

A nagging problem at Harwood offers another example. Supervisors were frustrated when experienced workers lost productivity and morale following transfers to new job assignments. For years the problem was interpreted primarily as one of individual attitude and "pressure" was applied with predictably miserable results (high tension, low productivity and moral, scapegoating). Lewin assessed the problem with his usual clarity and empathy, and to everyone's relief, conditions improved dramatically:

"There are indications that the transfer in these cases is indeed accompanied by a marked lowering of work morale in the sense of drive to higher production. If this interpretation is correct, learning after transfer should be slow, and indeed it is astonishingly slow. Although these workers are familiar with the machines, their speed improves so slowly that it is more profitable for the factory to hire new workers than to change the job of experienced workers.

Probably, several factors combine to decrease the force ...after transfer: a worker in good standing who is proud of his achievement is thrown back into a state of low working status. This is likely to affect his morale and eagerness. The goal of working at a level 'above standard' has been a realistic possibility before transfer; now it is 'too' high, it is out of reach. The studies on level of aspiration have shown that under these circumstances a person tends to 'give up.' This would explain the decrease...After group decision the learning curve rises, probably because the setting up of new goals brings about a resultant force toward higher levels without which learning may not take place (Lewin, 1947, 1997, p324)."

Although it is not documented, one hopes that CEO Marrow heeded the message about not moving experienced workers needlessly (which would then require on-going group interventions). Many employers today move workers because they want them to be "multi-skilled," and then are surprised when restraining forces impact their system in various ways.

The following case study, initiated to address conflict in a work group, nicely combines most of the elements of Lewin's approach to organization development. He begins the story near the end:

The accomplishments thus far may be summarized as follows: The mechanic and the supervisor who were ready to leave are back in the plant. The perception of all three fighting parties—the mechanic, the supervisor and the most critical, active group, the operators—who had been preoccupied with the issue of the "lie" and prestige has been turned toward the objective difficulties of production. Without any direct contact between the three parties, it has been established that their views of the production difficulties agree to a reasonable extent. All individuals involved have freely and without pressure expressed their agreement to some future steps. All three parties are in good and friendly rapport with the psychologist.

The procedure of the psychologist is based on the hypothesis that the permanent conflict is at least partly the result of some faulty organization of production. Therefore, before a remedy can be found the production procedure has to be analyzed realistically and sufficiently deeply to lay open the source of the difficulty.

The group lowest in the factory hierarchy is made the foundation for the factfinding...because these operators are most immediately affected and should be most realistically aware of at least some aspects of the problem. Then too, since the operators have a lower position in the factory hierarchy any rule suggested by the authorities, or even a view presented by them as a "fact," is likely to be felt by the operators as something of an imposition. **To gain their wholehearted co-operation later on it seems best to start the detailed fact-finding here, and it is also necessary to have the first suggestions for the new rules of production worked out by this group.**

Not all the operators but only those who did the most complaining were consulted. This seems strange if one considers that those operators who have less inclination for "trouble-making" are likely to give a more objective picture of the situation. The trouble-makers were made the cornerstone of the investigation since they are particularly important for the group dynamics in the factory.

Furthermore, **if those operators who usually did not make trouble were to initiate a solution, the trouble-makers would probably resist, feeling that they had been first left out and later pushed into something.**

The psychologist as leader of the group discussion presents the problem as an objective question of production procedure. The fact that he has no difficulty in holding the group's attention on this aspect of the situation indicates that **the preliminary interviews have set the stage for this perception** (my bolding) (Lewin, 1944, 1997, p97).

So many pearls of wisdom—the engagement of "the group lowest in the factory hierarchy"—the engagement of the "trouble-makers"—Lewin was brilliant at turning restraining forces into driving forces. The final comment—"that the preliminary interviews have set the stage for this perception" —is another gem. I'm not sure how I learned it (probably from dad), but it is common practice for me to use preliminary interviews mostly to establish relationships and the beginnings of trust, and to begin influencing how the people I am serving think about the challenges they are facing. To only a small degree am I in the "expert mode," i.e., there to gather information and adjust my basic "prescription." My prescription already is that some form of democratic principles/action research is going to both address the presenting problem and help develop the organization. I am there primarily to connect and begin to teach a new social construction of reality. This is exactly how Lewin's psychologist, Bavelas, begins:

"This attempt to change perception by an 'action interview' (as distinguished from a mere 'fact-finding interview') is one of the basic elements of treatment. By reorienting (the mechanic's and the supervisor's) perception from the field of personal emotional relationship to the same field of 'objective' facts, the life-spaces which guide the action of these persons have

become more similar although the persons themselves are not yet aware of this similarity (my bolding) (Lewin, 1944, 1997 p97)."

Lewin continues: "Fact-finding in this method is consciously used as a first step of action. The psychologist's or expert's knowing the facts does not have any influence unless these data are 'accepted as facts' by the group members. **Here lies a particular advantage of making the fact-finding a group endeavor. Coming together to discuss the facts and set up a plan is already an endeavor in co-operative action. It goes a long way to establish the atmosphere of co-operation, openness, and confidence toward which this procedure strives.** Although the mechanic and the supervisor do not participate directly in the group discussion of the operators, we have seen that the psychologist was very careful to involve them actively in the total scheme of fact-finding and planning (my bolding) (Lewin, 1944, 1997, p104)."

Finally, the conflict is approached as a symptom of group dynamics, especially the field of forces pertaining to production:

"**The realistic demands of production have to be satisfied in a way which conforms with the nature of group dynamics. To bring about a permanent solution it does not suffice to create amicable relations.**

The conflict described arose out of an aspect of production where overlapping authorities existed in a cognitively unclear situation. **The procedure is guided to an equal degree by the consideration of production and the problem of social relations.** As to details, one might mention the following points. The factory work can be seen as a process in which the speed is determined by certain driving and restraining forces. The production process runs through certain 'channels' as determined by the physical and social setting, particularly by certain 'rules' and by the authorities in power (management).

To increase production one can try to increase the driving forces by higher incentives or pressure, or try to weaken those forces that keep production down. The procedure described here follows the latter possibility. It tries to eliminate certain conflicts within the group and certain psychological forces acting on a key individual (the mechanic) which deter his efforts (my bolding) (Lewin, 1944, 1997, p102)."

By engaging the group in action research, production and morale increased, and *tension around the presenting problem decreased to a level where it was no longer relevant* because real problems of production that were increasing tension were addressed, while the social construction of reality had been simultaneously altered:

"It might be worthwhile to note that the original issue —namely, the lie and the resulting threat of quitting by the mechanic and the supervisor seems to have evaporated into thin air without ever having been treated directly. It seems that with a change in perception of the situation from that of a power problem to that of factory production, the lie issue, in the beginning a hard fact blocking smooth-running factory life, has lost the character of a 'fact.' This itself can be taken as a symptom of how deep and real the change of the perception and the psychological situation of all parties concerned has been (Lewin, 1944, 1997, p105)."

Using similar methods, I have seen similar changes time and again. Lewin didn't try to get everyone to "get along." Instead, he engaged the entire group in solving their common dilemmas of production. In the process, training on being more objective about work relationships eroded the strong judgments and feelings being held, while progress on production issues grounded in a real increase in the ability to influence built trust and improved morale.

In *Frontiers in Group Dynamics*, Lewin, again with clear non-blaming clarity, summarizes group dynamics at Harwood this way (Lewin, 1947, 1997, p319):

Production in a Factory

The output of a factory as a whole or of a work-team frequently shows a relatively constant level of output through an extended period of time. It can be viewed as a quasi-stationary equilibrium. An analysis of the relevant forces is of prime importance for understanding and planning changes.

One of the forces keeping production down is the strain of hard or fast work. There is an upper ceiling for human activity. For many types of work the force away from the strain... increases faster the closer one comes to the upper limit. The force field has probably a gradient similar to an exponential curve.

The common belief views the desire to make more money (fP, m) as the most important force toward higher production levels. To counter the gradient of the forces...away from fast work, various incentive systems are used which offer higher rates of pay above a certain standard.

Several reasons make it unlikely that the force toward greater output is actually proportional to the unit pay rate. An increase in earning a certain amount means quite different things to different people. Some factories which moved from a northern state to the South ten years ago found it impossible for years to reach a level of production which was at all comparable to that of northern workers. One of the reasons was the fact that for the rural southern girls the weekly pay was so much above previous living standards that they did not care to make more money even for a relatively small additional effort.

In teamwork one of the strongest forces is the desire to remain not too far above or below the rest of the group. This holds particularly between "parallel workers" or "friends" in an assembly line. An important force against increase of speed may be the fear that a temporary increase of speed would bring about pressure from the supervisor or foreman permanently to keep up the higher speed (my bolding).

In the following graphic (Figure 11.2), yet another group sets and achieves a higher standard, and then sustains it:

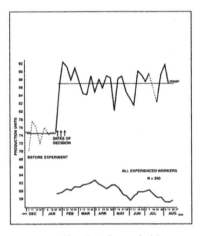

The effect of group decision on
sewing machine operators.

Figure 11.2
The effect of group decision...(Lewin, 1948, 1999, p283)

The same principles and methods apply to inter-group behavior (and pave the way for effective "whole system" interventions): "It seems to be impossible to predict group behavior without taking into account group goals, group standards, group values, and the way a group 'sees' its own situation and that of other groups. Group conflicts would have quite different solutions if the various groups concerned did not perceive differently the situation existing at a given time (Lewin, 1947, 1997, p308)." I'll say more on cross-group and whole systems interventions in Chapter 13.

Finally, Lewin offers a word of caution to those who think one solution fits all (or that they can replicate his results without understanding his methods):

"One should be slow in generalizing experimental findings. Any type of organization like a factory, a business enterprise, a community center, a school system, or the Army has characteristics of its own. **What democracy means technically has to be determined in each organization in line with its particular objective** (my bolding) (Lewin, 1944, 1999, p290)."

Involving the people "locally" in doing their own action research is the best way to make that determination.

Let us turn now to a practitioner's past, present, and future application of Lewinian methods of planned change.

Section IV
Planned Change Now

Lewin commemorative plaque in Mogilno, Poland

Chapter 12
T-groups and OD

"...it is easier to affect deeply the personality of **10 people if they can be melted into a group** than to affect the personality of any one individual treated separately (my bolding) (Lewin, 1943, 1999, p334)."

Robert Crosby working at a flip chart during a T-group workshop

As described in Chapter 9, the Connecticut workshop gave birth to the T-group—a group process where the group members openly assess their own behavior and that of the other group members, including the leaders, *and* the group dynamics as the process unfolds. Lewin and his associates immediately began visualizing an evolution of that experience. They secured funding and a location for their "cultural island" at the Gould Academy in Bethel, Maine. They rethought the process so that instead of having evening debriefs, feedback and debriefs of moments in the process would happen in that moment ("here and now") or as close to the moment as possible. The processing of the process and of the group dynamics *was to be the process*, not a separate event. Training in planned change and skill practice (especially via role play) would also occur. It was a bold and powerful design.

The experiment, to be called a Basic Skills Training (BST) group, was a core element of a three-week workshop conducted in the summer of 1947. Sadly, Lewin passed away before this first evolution in T-group learning would occur.

Ron Lippitt says this about that initial session of what came to be known as the National Training Laboratory (or NTL):

"Three years ago the National Training Laboratory in Group Development was organized specifically as a training center for teams which would take leadership in action-training-research projects in the fields of education, industry, government, social work, labor, religious work, volunteer organizations, and community life (Lippitt, 1949, p262)." Note the intention of *developing teams* that could then provide a force field of support for individuals, at both the 1946 workshop and in this initial description of NTL.

By 1948 Benne reports that, "Some participants went home feeling that they were qualified to conduct human relations training. Where their previous education did not warrant this claim, a few participants carried out inadequate training projects... It was not until 1955 that a special advanced program for the development of trainers was instituted at Bethel (Bradford et al, 1964, p87)." Dad attended that advanced program, facilitated by Lippitt, Bradford, and Benne, in 1958.

The tendency of enthusiastic participants attempting to lead T-group processes would cause trouble in the years to come. Having provided advanced training to a number of facilitators and would-be facilitators over the years, including my friend and colleague Cotton Mears (see the dedication), I can tell you that it is easier said than done, requires co-facilitating many groups, and that not everyone is cut out to be a T-group facilitator even if they have strong academic credentials and other relevant experience.

T-group leadership requires strong democratic principles, a la Lewin: "Only through practical experience can one learn that peculiar democratic combination of conduct which includes responsibility toward the group, ability to recognize differences of opinion, without considering the other person a criminal, and readiness to accept criticism in a matter of fact way while offering criticism with sensitivity for the other person's feeling (Lewin, 1943, 1997, p45)." T-group facilitation, in the model my father has taught me, is not for those with laissez-faire inclinations.

Dad was exposed to T-group learning during those early years, with his first experience coming at Boston University in 1953. As father puts it, Boston University is "in sight" of both MIT and Harvard, and somehow his first T-group trainer and mentor, Dr. Walter Holcomb, had been exposed to Lewin's circle and the methodology. "When I asked Professor Holcomb for a course about group dynamics he said, 'This course is *in* group dynamics, not *about*.' I would soon deeply admire Professor Holcomb. I nodded my head without, I realized later, having the slightest idea about what he meant. My first T-group! Soon would follow my second (Crosby, 2019, p8)!"

By 1965 my father was working with and being mentored by Dr. Goodwin Watson, a colleague of both Lewin (with whom he was involved in the Commission for Community Interrelations) and Dewey, and he had begun his decades long mentoring by Dr. Lippitt. In 1966 he became an NTL Associate.

I add these details because dad has applied T-group methodology to adult learning and organization development throughout his long career (which continues to this day) and he is the primary source of my own professional training. He was also intimately familiar with the early years of NTL.

During those same years, T-groups became "the latest, hottest management fad," with over twenty thousand businessmen attending NTL workshops by 1966 (Kleiner, 2008, p33). Adding to those numbers were the growing ranks of OD practitioners. In the early years of OD, almost all practitioners went through extensive T-group training as part of their professional development. Indeed, a primary intent of the NTL T-groups was to develop "change agents." As Bradford et al put it in 1964, an "essential" focus was: "Focus on Self as an Agent of Change. Unless the individual perceives his need for continued learning and growth and accepts personal responsibility for initiating steps towards learning, unless he has reduced internal barriers and blocks to his learning, and unless he has learned to receive help from others and to give help to others in processes of changing, little continuing learning or change will take place in himself or in the social systems of which he is a part outside the laboratory. The training laboratory assists the participant to see himself, actually and potentially, as an agent of change (Bradford et al, 1964, p47)."

As Gandhi put it, to be a change agent you must "Be the change you wish to see in the world."

"Use of self," honed in no better way than through T-group learning, becomes part of the organization development process. Edgar Schein gives the following example: "...Ralston, the division director, was gradually learning to see how his own behavior as a strong 'parent' was perceived by his adult department heads both as a source of inspiration and strength and sometimes as overbearing and demeaning. Ralston would cause the second perception particularly when he lectured and overkilled points, something he sometimes did to me so I could see how it felt.

At one point in our relationship I found myself giving him direct feedback on what this behavior was doing to me; this rather unfroze him and made him begin to consider alternatives. He decided he would listen more, especially at meetings...

At first he had to practice this behavior on me and get comfortable with it himself. When he began to do it at meetings he received strong post-meeting confirmation from me, and, once his department heads overcame their surprise, they let him know as well how much his new approach was appreciated. At this point the new behavior was beginning to be refrozen (Schein, 1987, p111)."

Use of self—paying attention to your own experience as a source of data and effectively giving and receiving feedback —is indispensable to OD. T-group learning remains the most direct path I know of for gaining such skills—skills which are critical for leadership and effective influence in any relationship or system. In case it is not obvious, I am an unapologetic advocate of T-group learning, *if the T-group is effectively led.*

That is not a given. As Kleiner documents, T-groups became a hugely popular fad. Quality control was perhaps impossible under the circumstances. A legion of facilitators tried their hand at running T-groups, many no doubt sincerely wanting to replicate what had been an important and positive experience, and many likewise drawn by the lure of providing a service that was in demand. A facilitator has to make a living, right? Eventually too many were run without the necessary clarity, and too many stories emerged of ugly confrontations and traumatic experiences. The fad lost its luster, and with the exception of my father, NTL, Tavistock, a handful of OD graduate programs, and a few other professional pockets, the use of the method receded and almost faded away.

NTL handled some of the fallout by only allowing strangers to attend their workshops, so as to avoid disruption of work relationships and assure safety for individual learning. My father is the only facilitator I know of who consistently ran T-groups with work teams and in industrial settings undeterred by the surge and contraction of T-groups as a fad. His capacity to do so was rooted in a clear vision of the methodology, grounded in Lewin's original intent.

Let me recap the elements of T-group learning present at the beginning of the 1946 workshop, and add those that emerged during that workshop and after:

1. T-groups are conducted in the form of a workshop, typically lasting at least a week (the original workshops in 1946 and in 1947 lasted two weeks).

2. There may be multiple groups in the workshop (working together at times and working separately at times).

3. A skilled facilitator leads each group.

4. The participants are taught practical theory and skills such as communication and conflict management.

5. Behavioral observation is built into the process.

6. Teams are included so as to leverage group dynamics in sustaining the learning after the workshop.

The following is based on what emerged during the 1946 workshop:

7. Like the original moment where a participant challenged the faculty's version of events, participants are encouraged to give feedback to the T-group facilitator(s). As one of the original participant's noted, once this happens (assuming the facilitator handles it in a way that encourages further feedback) the door is opened for others to challenge the authority figures, to give an increasing amount of feedback to their peers, and to solicit feedback about their own behavior.

8. As per Lewin and his staff's intention for the T-group workshop the following year, the "Immediate experiences of participants furnish the basic ingredients for laboratory learning (Bradford et al, 1964, p46)."

9. The 1947 focus on teaching change agent skills applies to anyone trying to influence their primary systems (in other words, everybody).

Dad was able to retain all of that focus and refine the methods of observation, feedback, and learning. His design provided enough psychological safety that people who worked together could tolerate the process, and indeed were likely to strengthen their relationships instead of damaging them. Because we have worked in many systems for years on end and even for decades, we have strong firsthand knowledge to support this claim.

The Interpersonal Gap by Dr. John Wallen (Appendix A), which was unavailable to Lewin and his immediate protégés (simply because Wallen didn't develop it until 1964), strengthened father's design. Wallen and dad were colleagues, leading many T-groups together, and the gap model soon became a linchpin of the process. The clarity in Wallen's model about what is behavior and what is interpretation helps people quickly refine their feedback skills and take ownership in their interactions. The participants in our process become more disciplined participant observers of themselves and others. This reduces inflammatory and blaming statements, and helps the process unfold in a manner that pushes learning while providing enough psychological safety. It also creates a guideline for the facilitators, who apply the same methods and behaviors to themselves that they are teaching to the participants. I have no doubt that Lewin would have loved Wallen's theory, as a powerful foundation for the following:

"The first task of science is to register objectively and describe reliably the material one wishes to study...

Social Perception and Interpretation

One of the fundamental difficulties is related to the distinction between "observation" and "interpretation." In all sciences, it is important to keep observation as free as possible from theories and subjective interpretation. In psychology, too, the observer has to learn to use his eyes and ears and to report what happened rather than what he thinks should have happened according to his preconceived ideas. That is not an easy task (Lewin, 1943, 1997, p279)."

Wallen's theory fulfills this need: "The other (empirical basis) should be a progressively deeper understanding of the laws of 'social perception' (Lewin, 1943, 1999, p339)." And Wallen's theory further provides a firm foundation for this: "All observation, finally, means classifying certain events under certain categories. Scientific reliability depends upon correct perception and correct classification. Here again the observers have to be trained and trained correctly (Lewin, 1943, 1997, p 281)."

With everyone learning the skills of objective *participant observation*, T-groups, effectively led, remain a unique process wherein participants learn from what is actually emerging from moment to moment within them and between them and the rest of the group. In our model, that includes their reactions to the facilitator, which we invite them to be open about, and which we respond to in the same genuine, open, and respectful manner we are trying to instill. Participants are then able to work in the here-and-now on their reactions to authority figures, and begin to establish as much of an adult-to-adult pattern of relating as possible.

Facilitated effectively, the T-group process encourages open mindedness in a unique way. *It works directly on the social construction of reality.* This is essential for sustainable individual, group, and organizational development. In Benne's words: "The world in which we act is the world as we perceive it. Changes in knowledge or changes in beliefs and value orientation will not result in action changes unless changed perceptions of self and situation are achieved...Habitual perceptions are challenged by open exchange of feedback between members of a group as they share their different responses to the 'same' events. If a member attaches positive valence to other members of the group or to the group as a whole, he can accept the different perceptions of other members as genuine phenomenological alternatives to his own ways of perceiving self and world. He may then try to perceive and feel the world as others in his group perceive and feel it. In the process, his own perceptual frames may be modified or at least recognized as belonging to him and operating as one among many other constructions of social reality (Benne, 1976, p35)."

Opening one's mind is no small accomplishment. It is our hypothesis, supported by decades of client outcomes, that systems that incorporate T-group learning are able to decrease their negative and blaming perceptions of individuals and groups, and thus handle challenges and change more calmly and effectively.

Gilmore Crosby (left) and Chris Crosby during a T-group based workshop

Our OD model heavily relies on T-group learning as the training portion of Lewin's training-action-research. In a properly facilitated T-group, people become more effective at being the way they want to be in a group and in a larger system, and in understanding and influencing group dynamics. As Benne put it: "...it takes time and effort for a group to learn a method of experimental inquiry where their own feelings, perceptions, commitments, and behaviors are the data to be processed in the inquiry (Benne, 1976, p35)." It is *action research by the group members* as they experiment with changing themselves and influencing others.

Father's successful adaptation of T-groups to industrial workforces has also succeeded in no small part due to his ability to relate to all humans as peers and to apply the same behavioral standards to self that we are imparting to others. It also helps build rapport when participants with less power in the system see the facilitators holding people with more power in the system to the same or even higher standards of feedback and behavioral conduct. The people with more power for the most part are appreciative of getting live coaching as well. Too many people in the system handle them with kid gloves. As Lewin puts it: "The normal gap between teacher and student... can...be a real obstacle to acceptance of the advocated conduct (Lewin, 1945, 1997, p55)." For a facilitator to be effective, that gap has to be reduced.

As Lewin noted, for change to take hold and stick people must feel free to openly share concerns, conflicts, pessimism, doubts (including distrust of the OD facilitator which is likely in the beginning of any intervention), and reactions to the leadership. True freedom of expression also includes appreciation, which should be encouraged (it is often underdone) but not at the expense of other thoughts and feelings. A culture that can tolerate and insist on the full range of expression is a culture that will bond (freeze) and remain resilient in the face of adversity. T-group learning gets to the heart of all of the above.

T-group participants in a leadership development program (debriefing an experience)

There are many sources for learning more about our T-group methodology (none better than father's most recent book, *Memoirs of a Change Agent*). I'm not going to go into further detail here. However, I do want to share the following story, based on true events, of a T-group workshop in an industrial setting:

The T-Group based workshop has just begun. The 24 participants and 3 faculty members have introduced themselves, and the CEO (who is participating himself) has briefly explained why he has sponsored this week-long workshop and its follow-up session. The plant he runs has been losing money for years, and he believes that the people must learn a new way to work together if the plant is to survive. Relationships are tense throughout the organization, especially between management and labor. Because of his trust in the facilitators, the CEO has taken the risk of inviting twelve members of the Union leadership, including the president, who is barely on speaking terms with the CEO, along with eleven other members of the plant leadership team. There are formal and informal layers of reporting relationships in the mix, and years of animosity. As the participants sit in a large circle (unencumbered by tables) to begin the week, there is no escaping the initial awkwardness. The Union President chooses to stand near the door, in his own words "uncertain" as to whether he will stay.

The workshop, and a broader OD strategy, is designed to help the organization decrease tension while increasing business performance. The facilitator has already worked with the management team on their own group dynamics and, with his colleagues, will be working with every team in the organization during the weeks and months to come. He has also met with the Union leadership, both to show respect, to inform, and to allow them to get their own feel for the OD strategy and his team of facilitators. It doesn't hurt that one of the facilitators used to be an electrician in a manufacturing plant.

Following the CEO's kickoff, the lead facilitator asks the participants to talk in pairs. Working in pairs is a critical part of the workshop structure. He explains that they will be doing this a lot throughout the week, and they will be learning as much from each other as they will from the facilitators. He even walks the room, saying, "So you two are a pair, and you two, and you two," etc., to assure that pairing occurs. The task is to talk about what they just heard...what they think and feel about it. Instantly 50% of the room goes from being quiet to being verbal. This simple structure is repeated throughout the week, with different pairings, and is a big asset both to learning and to decreasing stress. Lewin knew that group change was more powerful than individual change...pairing brings peer-to-peer influence to life, while also allowing some privacy for processing one's experience. In these workshops, people quickly get it that they are all peers in being human, even while they have different roles in the organization.

Now the room is buzzing with talk. The facilitator regains attention and invites anyone to speak. After an anxious silence, the conversation with the CEO begins. People admit their fears, "You guys are just here to brainwash us," and their hopes "We need to work together so maybe this will help." The CEO admits that he doesn't have all the answers, and that he and the management team had made some mistakes. The HR Director explains why he thinks the workshop is needed. The Union VP says, "I don't know what he just said, but I'm against it!" The room goes silent. The HR Director begins to fight back. The facilitator says something like, "This is a good example of why we are here" and manages to lighten the mood without taking sides. Even though the facilitator is working for his customer (the CEO), neutrality when helping with interactions is vital to effective facilitation. Everyone relaxes. The president chooses to stay. The workshop proceeds.

While it is possible to stubbornly stay outside the learning process during one of our workshops, it isn't easy. This is in no small way due to the brilliance of Lewin's understanding of group dynamics. It's hard to stay separate when your peers are participating, and even harder when the peer pressure is coming in the privacy of paired conversations. Most people are willing to give the process a chance, and the next thing you know, people are learning about themselves and trying on new behavior! It's tough to resist.

The same was true during the management-labor workshop above. The process was rolling along, and then sometime shortly after the *Active Listening Skills* theory session, a critical incident occurred. Sitting in the same T-group, and talking to each other directly, the Union President looked the CEO in the eye and said, "I don't usually listen to you when we talk. I'm just wrapped up in what I am wanting to say." The CEO said, "I do the same thing. I don't listen to what you are actually saying either." From that moment on they made a commitment to actually listen to each other and to be honest if they don't think it is happening. They shifted from adversaries to collaborators for the remainder of that president's term, and the entire plant shifted into a more collaborative direction. It wasn't just a critical incident for the workshop...it was transformational for the organization.

Amongst many emergent joint management and labor strategies that followed, they also became co-sponsors for a series of T-group based workshops, and the Union President became a reference for our work.

When a critical mass in an organization increases their capacity to foster a productive and safe work environment by giving clear direction, taking a stand for what they believe in, holding themselves and others accountable, fostering communication up and down the hierarchy, managing conflict, connecting with emotional intelligence (EQ) to all levels of the organization, and continually developing themselves, others, and the organization, high performance as measured by industry metrics follows. Participants consistently say T-group learning enriches their personal and professional lives. My hope is that T-group learning, with proper discipline, once again becomes a *movement* (from *T-Groups Adapted for the Workplace*, a soon-to-be-published article by Gilmore Crosby).

We come now to the final chapter of this book, a description of the OD approach built by my father based on Lewin's methods.

Chapter 13
The Past, Present, and Future of Planned Change

My intent in writing this final chapter is to offer examples of application of Lewin's theory and methods so that you, the reader, are as equipped as possible to pursue your own planned change. I recognize that another worthy effort would be to draw from many sources of application. That would be an entirely different and significant research effort. For now I have chosen to focus on the application history and methods I know. I hope the reader will forgive me for the extent to which this chapter pays tribute to my father's Lewinian legacy and OD practices.

At first a student of the methods himself, father has none-the-less been employing Lewinian methods since the 1960s, when Ron Lippitt recognized him as a "change agent (Crosby, 2019, p8)." I call that an understatement. When I was a kid, in segregated Nashville, I was in integrated church camps run by my father where we were in facilitated group processes where pale skinned ("white") kids like me had conversations with darker skinned ("black") kids. Fast forward to the 1970s and I am in an experimental school started by my father, with T-group learning as the kickoff for the opening year. At the same time, he also started an OD graduate program based on T-group learning (the Leadership Institute of Spokane... LIOS... morphing later into the Leadership Institute of Seattle).

Meanwhile, his application of Lewinian methods to OD was moving full speed ahead. To make a long story short, in one of his many OD books, *Cultural Change in Organizations*, dad, conveying his methods through a fictional customer named Peter (based on real events) summarizes his OD strategy this way (numbers added):

Peter's Change Strategy

- Leader sets *measurable* goals.
- Help direct reports *align* with the goals and be open to feedback.
- If your workplace has a union, work closely with union leaders and hourly employees to understand the goals.
- Communicate the goals across the organization in small groups through a *dialogue*.
- Expect the leaders of intact groups (boss and direct reports) to sharpen their goals with input from their direct reports.
- Cascade a group process in each intact workgroup as taught in Chapter 3 (of *Cultural Change in Organizations*). Process must include clarity of goals, generation of issues and solutions, and follow-up.
- Work with the company's most important cross-functional (matrixed) projects and ongoing, cross-functional tasks.
- Develop a critical mass of strategic employees with high interactive skills who have the capacity to take a stand and stay connected, deal constructively with disagreements/conflict, be decisive, and stay the course against resistance.
- Develop a team (cadre) of key people trained in the strategic engagement activities in this book who will help sustain the shift in culture and alignment around the leader's goals.

Peter realized he could easily turn this into a program—a new "flavor of the month"—rather than developing effective leadership.

- He reviewed the "Eleven Do's And Don'ts For Those Who Are Serious About Change" (*Appendix A, Cultural Change in Organizations*).

- He re-read "What It Takes To Pull Off a Cultural Change" (*Appendix C, Cultural Change in Organizations*).

- He committed, in a new way, to follow up. The words "You are not serious about change until you are serious about follow-up" helped Peter realize he had been too passive when conducting follow-up. He committed to hold himself and his direct reports to higher standards and instructed them to do the same throughout the organization.

- He reaffirmed the need to have skilled internal or external staff doing day-by-day nurturing until his cadre was developed. They would then sustain the ongoing change that is constantly needed in a productive environment: managing emerging conflicts, making continuous contributions to work-process improvement, ensuring decision and role clarity, encouraging accurate data flow, and fostering authentic healthy interaction.

In Appendix B in this book, a case study of our culture change work at PECO Nuclear, I summarize the same OD strategy this way:

1. Clarify goals and cascade alignment.

2. Develop a critical mass of employees with high interactive skills.

3. Reinforce goal alignment and continuous improvement conversations in all intact teams.

4. Drive cultural change through key cross-functional projects.

5. Create a "cadre" of key line people early in the process who can help facilitate the change.

The author and Robert P. Crosby, 1981

Meanwhile, notice that T-groups aren't mentioned directly in "*Peter's Strategy*" (although they are implied in bullet #8). My first OD work, overseen by my father back in 1984, included no T-group work. Instead it involved working with every group in three Contadina tomato processing plants. First there was a two-day "kickoff" session for the entire plant (production is seasonal so they could actually all be in the same room together). The CEO talked about his strategy for improving the business unit, including targeted metrics. Dad then trained for two days to set the stage for effective use of the survey sessions. Each group then met (with wet behind the ears me facilitating every group in two of the plants, while dad handled the third) using dad's computerized survey (which was a big deal at the time) to do a self-assessment, action planning, and implementation. Every group in all three plants were simultaneously working on improvement of their internal production issues (including safety, quality, etc.) and team dynamics, and their inter-group and process dynamics! The survey-feedback process he designed is the epitome of action research (and incorporates bullets 1-6). I still use it on a regular basis today. As Lippitt said to my father and his colleague (and mine) Dr. John Scherer, "They who put their pencil to the survey paper should also see and work the data (Crosby, 2019, p197)." As per Lewin's wise instructions, we let the people facing the problem figure out what to do, including working with the leadership to design the OD strategy.

There are, of course, no simultaneous control groups in a normal OD intervention. Such a research method is rather hard to justify when you are being paid to improve the organization ("Do you mind if we let these groups flounder so we can compare the results?"). Admittedly, as practitioners our action research is conducted mostly to assist the client system. Testing and improving our own methods, and adding to the body of knowledge of the social sciences, while important, are definitely secondary considerations. That being said, I'm excited about the contribution that this book represents, hopefully bringing many people back full circle to the solid roots of planned change.

Instead of research methods such as control groups, our OD strategy measures results by the organization's own before and after metrics. Periodic survey data can add another barometer. Indeed, dad used survey data coupled with performance metrics to verify that teams with strong group dynamics (such as the relationship between the group and the supervisor) correlate with high validity to strong performance on safety, quality, productivity, etc. With these methods, micro and macro performance before and after OD interventions becomes the "control group."

During my time as an internal OD Specialist with PECO Nuclear in the mid-nineties, I turned the annual employee survey into a system-wide action research process. Every work team, with the help of skilled facilitation, got their own data and came up with their own solutions. Of course, I couldn't work with every team myself, so as per dad's strategy (and true to Lewin's value of transferring skills to the front lines) I developed an internal "cadre" from all levels of the hierarchy to facilitate survey feedback sessions, with me taking on the executives and the most difficult groups (my list #5, Peter's bullet #9).

Surveys are no magic bullet if they are not coupled with effective action research methods. As father put it: "We know what does not work. It does not work to survey people and not show them the results. It also does not work to survey people and have top management or an outside expert develop recommendations (prescriptions). It does not work to survey people and have a general session where results are reported and nothing visible to the employees is done. These approaches have all been tried hundreds of times and have, with rare exceptions, been found wanting. People tend to become irritable and defensive, with a resulting lowered morale and decreased work efficiency (Crosby, 2019, p196)."

In contrast, facilitated survey feedback immediately teaches democratic leadership and followership principles. By itself it goes a long way in fulfilling this aspect of Lewin's vision: "There is no question but that the culture of individuals or small groups can be changed deeply in a relatively short time... Experiments with both children and adults prove that the social atmosphere of groups can be changed profoundly by introducing different forms of leadership (Lewin, 1943, 1997, p41)."

Much like at Harwood, where Lewin was sponsored wholeheartedly by CEO Alfred Marrow, dad's methods begin through collaboration and coaching of a leader who is high enough in the hierarchy that they can authorize and drive OD strategy into the organization. Part of that strategy is then to develop leadership skills at all layers, including the floor. Working with every intact work team as per the designs mentioned above is a fast and effective way to do "on the job" leadership and followership training. Running T-group based workshops, or leadership development programs based on T-groups is another. Indeed, dad designed and ran the Aluminum Company of America's (ALCOA) corporate leadership program for fifteen years. More than 50 hourly unionized employees participated, including the late great Cotton Mears (to whom this book is dedicated). Although working with actual work groups is one important part of our strategy, including at times doing T-group work with intact teams, we prefer mixing layers and functions of the organization in most of our T-group based interventions. The quality of the conversation that goes on between hourly workers and executives in a well-run T-group is often transformational for both parties and for the organization.

Leadership development as part of culture change is fundamental in our OD model and supported by Lewin's thinking and research. As he put it in *The Special Case of Germany* (Lewin, 1943, 1997, p43-45):

Techniques of Changing Culture

1. *Satisfaction is not enough...*
2. *Some general positive principles...*(a)The change has to be a change of group atmosphere...(b)It can be shown that the system of values which governs the ideology of a group is dynamically linked with other power aspects within the life of the group...(c)...a change in methods of leadership is probably the quickest way to bring about a change in the cultural atmosphere of a group.
3. *The change from autocracy to democracy.* Experiments on groups and leadership training suggest the following conclusions:

(a) The change of a group atmosphere from autocracy or laissez-faire to democracy through a democratic leader amounts to a re-education of the followers toward "democratic followership." Any group atmosphere can be conceived of as a pattern of role playing. Neither the autocratic nor the democratic leader can play his role without the followers being ready to play their role accordingly...

(b) The experiments show that this shift in roles cannot be accomplished by a "hands off" policy. To apply the principle of "individualistic freedom" merely leads to chaos... to be able to change a group atmosphere toward democracy **the democratic leader has to be in power and has to use his power** for active re-education.

(c)...lecture and propaganda do not suffice to bring about the necessary change... For larger groups, this means that a hierarchy of leaders has to be trained which reaches into all essential sub-parts of the group.

(d)...Democratic leaders cannot be trained autocratically; it is on the other hand of utmost importance that the trainer of democratic leaders establish and hold his position of leadership. It is, furthermore, very important that the people who are to be changed from another atmosphere toward democracy be dissatisfied with the previous situation and feel the need for a change. There are indications that it is easier to change an unsatisfied autocratic leader toward democratic techniques than to change a laissez-faire type of leader or a satisfied half-democratic leader (my bolding).

It's a shame that Lewin wasn't able to do his own experiments in leadership development by applying T-groups to industry. Thankfully father, and a few rare others, carried that torch and kept it burning brightly. In our work everything above holds true, including that last sentence. It is far easier to coach a driving type of leader towards effectiveness (as in Schein's example in

Chapter 12 of teaching them to listen) than to coach a more "hands off" or introverted leader towards engagement, clarity of expectations, giving and seeking feedback, monitoring of performance, and the like. It can be done, but it is harder and takes more time. Both of course require a light bulb going on inside the individual in terms of seeing a genuine payoff to making a change. T-groups, coaching and facilitation of leadership interactions with their direct reports all increase the voltage to that inner light.

Hopefully if you have read this far lightbulbs are going off in your own head about the many possible applications of Lewin's planned change in your own life and work. Dad's adaption is worthy of replication, but it is by no means the only version of Lewin-based OD. On the other hand, he is one of the only practitioners to consistently use T-groups in industry, academia, and other organizational settings, so if you are going to attempt that by all means you would be wise to avail yourself of our experience and knowledge, which we are more than willing to share. For step by step guidance on our general methods of OD (not including T-group facilitation, which can't be taught by simply reading a book), my brother's two volume set, *Strategic Engagement: Practical Tools to Raise Morale and Increase Results*, is an excellent resource.

Before I wrap this up, there is another important application of Lewinian theory to explore, the use of force field analysis. Dad especially applied field theory in an overt way when engaging in Peter's bullet #7 (my bullet #4). As he put it: *Work with the company's most important cross functional (matrixed) projects*. Business critical cross-functional projects such as a nuclear refueling outage or a major IT implementation are great opportunities to drive culture change throughout an organization (an opportunity missed by most). Goal clarity, role clarity, communication skills, conflict skills, can all be enhanced while implementing such a project. As in Lewin's integrated public housing, silos can be shattered. In our experience, along with these and other desired cultural outcomes, project performance measures such as safety, quality, on-time delivery, and cost control can be reliably met or exceeded.

Part of our process is a large system cross-functional planning session, which dad originally coined a Turnaround Implementation and Planning Intervention (or TIPI) when he first successfully applied it to a floundering nuclear refueling outage.

Early in the process the facilitator explains force field analysis, drawing a visual on a flip chart something like this:

Figure 13.1
Force field analysis (Schmuck, 2006, p11)

As per Lewin's advice, we engage the people in the room in a brainstorm-based analysis of any and all restraining forces, both social (such as mistrust) and technical (such as equipment needs) that are in the way. The non-blaming forced-listening dialogue that ensues is in itself transformational, although without a Lewian group decision process it would be a waste of time. Dad's design shifts the group dynamics into a driving force, while focusing the collective wisdom of the organization on addressing other restraining forces, instead of just repeating their habit of trying to shove in change.

TIPI participants at an industrial location

By the end of this design, not only is the organization engaged in action research to reduce the restraining forces threatening project implementation and other performance, but implementation responsibility is spread amongst the participants, including hourly workers who identify improvement ideas. In true Lewinian style yet another restraining force – management doing all the thinking, planning, communicating, and implementing – has been shifted through the intervention method itself. Engagement, limited to being an official "value" in most corporations (that scores low none-the-less in their annual surveys), becomes a structured reality overnight. Going explicitly after the restraining forces is an important reason why the process works.

Little did I realize for many years that the same can be said of the intact work group interventions and T-groups. To some degree the shifting of restraining forces—such as group mistrust of the facilitator, of management, and even of each other—into a driving force—through our genuine respect for how people are feeling and what they are thinking when we arrive (understandably cynical is a safe bet) and through consistent application and teaching of democratic principles - is woven into everything we do. Lewin and dad were/are both smart cookies.

And that, as they say, is a wrap.

Remember friends that planned change is a process of "Unfreezing, Moving, and Freezing of Group Standards (Lewin, 1947, 1997, p330)." In other words, if you want change to stick (i.e., freeze), you must change the environment (the primary groups to which an individual belongs). That is why leveraging group dynamics as a strategy of whole systems change is so powerful and will continue to be so.

$B = f(P,E)$ was radical when Lewin first said it. Nature versus nurture was a polarized debate. The debate is not over, especially in terms of the social construction of reality most people perceive through when problems emerge. Organizational cultures still lean towards focusing on and blaming individual performance (including individual groups, such as maintenance, production, front line supervision or entire locations) when there are problems (which there always are), instead of thinking systemically (where problems are viewed as a symptom of the total system). This element of socially constructed reality is in itself a restraining force that must be changed to decrease needless drama and defensiveness, and increase organizational performance. Lewin's formula supports an OD strategy in which individual and group change is linked and implemented simultaneously, thus reinforcing and sustaining one another.

My father's adaptation of Lewin applies training-action-research by engaging every work team in an organization or location in self-analysis and action planning using survey data, and by involving large cross-functional groups in analysis and action planning of whole systems problems. At age 24, under my father's mentorship, I was doing the same. The theory and methods are sound. I in turn have mentored many "lay" practitioners in cadres and otherwise who had nothing more going for them than a willingness to be led and faith in the process.

Dad believes as Lewin did that the people facing the

problems are the best people to solve them; they just need the leadership and structure to enable them to do it. From shortening the length of nuclear industry outages, to successful software implementation, to increasing retention rates of at-risk adolescents in school, to resolving a stalemate between citizens and a city government, I have yet to face a problem where OD grounded in action research doesn't provide fast and reliable progress.

Since there is persistent pressure these days for rapid improvement with minimal effort, let me emphasize *fast*. Whereas many consultants want to do a study, including a survey where they interpret the data before they develop recommendations, our application of action research often has work groups on day one doing a quick self-analysis (using ten survey questions as a stimulus for dialogue) and generating actions/commitments, some of which they begin to implement during the dialogue. Imagine a whole system of teams doing that, and you get the idea. If anyone can create faster (planned) change, I'd like to see it.

As Stephen King says, thank you dear reader. Writing this has been very educational and fulfilling for me. I hope reading it has been for you, and that you will use the methods and spread the word far and wide. It is possible to plan change. Don't let any gurus tell you otherwise. Having said that, always do your planning with Lewinian realism that challenges will emerge, and that you will have to persevere. Fortunately, you can apply social science to overcoming whatever lies ahead.

Lewin gave us these tools; let's not waste them. Let us instead build upon his methods and use social science to better ourselves and to create a more democratic and effective world within our workplaces and in our global community.

Appendix A
The Interpersonal Gap

Reprinted with permission from *Leadership Can Be Learned: Clarity, Connection, and Results*, by Gilmore Crosby.

Applied behavioral scientist Kurt Lewin, the founder of my profession (organization development), once said "There's nothing so practical as a good theory" (Lewin, 1943, 1999, p336). *The Interpersonal Gap* (Wallen, 1964) is one of the most practical theories of behavioral science, offering a transformational mix of awareness and behavioral skills. Self-awareness and the ability to tune in to others is a foundation of personal effectiveness, but awareness without skills is like a puzzle with half the pieces missing. By logically packaging awareness and skills in a practical manner, Wallen's theory perfectly supports both EQ and Friedman's leadership model.

According to Wallen, "The most basic and recurring problems in social life stem from what you intend and the actual effect of your actions on others" (Wallen, 1964, p1). I would add (and I'm confident Wallen would agree) that "basic and recurring problems" stem equally from the reverse: your own interpretations, sometimes accurate, sometimes not, of the intentions of others. While both their interpretation of you and your interpretation of them are worth paying attention to, it is the latter source of trouble over which you have the most potential control.

In short, Wallen's theory is that each of us has intentions in every interaction (we intend a certain impact), we translate (or encode) our intentions into words and actions, the people we are interacting with translate (decode) our words and actions, and the decoding determines the initial emotional impact on the receiver, as illustrated in Figure A.1:

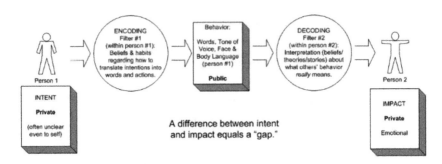

Figure A.1
The Interpersonal Gap

This process occurs constantly, and in a nanosecond. I react to you, and in that moment you are already reacting to my reactions. To further complicate things, our filters are complex and ever changing. Our history together, our separate life experiences, our culture, the nature of our relationship (i.e., roles such as boss and subordinate, parent and child, salesperson and customer, etc.) all impact our immediate filters about each other. There is ample potential for misunderstanding at any step in the process (beginning with the formidable task of understanding yourself—that is, with having clarity about what impact you really want in any given interaction). Such misunderstandings are what Wallen refers to as a "gap." As he puts it, "Interpersonal gap refers to the degree of congruence between one person's intentions and the effect produced in the other. If the effect is what is intended, the gap has been bridged. If the effect is the opposite of what was intended, the gap has become greater."

Wallen goes on to say, "We see our own actions in the light of our own intentions, but we see the other's actions not in the light of the other person's intentions but in the effect on us."

In other words, we usually know what we intended, especially when we believe we've been misunderstood (when we believe others have interpreted our words and actions differently than we intended). It is easy to notice Wallen's gap in those moments. That awareness is the first vital step in potentially clearing up such misunderstandings.

It's more problematic when the shoe is on the other foot: when you interpret another's words and actions in a manner that has an undesired effect on you.

Understanding the power your interpretations have on your own reactions is the starting point for increasing your objectivity and becoming less of a victim to your own interpretations. For example, a person who gives you "close supervision" (an interpretation in itself) may also be decoded/interpreted as (a) "not trusting your work" or (b) "being committed to you," [or (c), or (d), etc.]. A worker who speaks with anger may also be decoded/interpreted either as (a) "a troublemaker" or (b) "passionate about their job." The same behaviors, decoded differently, evoke different reactions (emotions, beliefs, etc.). Simple but hard to remember when the (emotional) heat is on, especially since your circle of associates will likely agree with your negative interpretations, lending what seems like validity to your judgments about the other person or group (thus reinforcing the systems dynamics of herding, triangulation, and homeostasis). And the subtle tension fueled by such negative beliefs makes it likely that future interactions will further reinforce the current outcomes.

Does this mean that you should never have negative judgments of others? Absolutely not. Besides the fact that such a suspension of interpretation would be virtually unachievable, it would be undesirable as well. Honest and timely critical feedback is a vital factor in a high-performance workplace. What it does mean in a nutshell is that it is wise to avoid using needlessly inflammatory judgments ("You're not a team player"), while it is useful to be as skillful as possible in describing the behavior that led to your interpretations of others (especially if you are an authority figure giving them performance feedback!). Equally important, it is wise to leave ample room for questioning your interpretations.

In other words, don't get so attached to your interpretations that you defend them and close your mind to other possibilities. If you are being objective, you will understand that your initial interpretation of someone's words and actions may be very different than what they meant. Close gaps by being specific about what you think they said or did (keeping in mind that they may not describe their words and deeds the same way), and about the emotional impact your interpretation of their words and actions is having on you. The good news is you have the ability to reconsider your own interpretations, and that is a critical step for breaking any patterns of misunderstanding that are needlessly complicating your relationships at home and at work.

Wallen states: "I know myself by my intentions; I know others by their _____."

How would you finish the sentence? Think of your response, and then continue reading.

If you said, "I know others by their actions/behavior," your answer reflects the dominant cultural perspective of our times. In other words, most people would give that answer. It is part of the personality theory culture we spoke about earlier. "I know them by their actions; for things to be different, they have to be different." It follows that your efforts will be on analyzing them and trying to change them (or getting rid of them). And since the people around you are operating in the same cultural mode (answering the question the same way), that seems to validate your perspective. It also means that when there is tension, it is likely they will be analyzing your personality flaws, similar to how you are analyzing them. This cultural paradigm does more damage than good.

Wallen's completion of that sentence, on the other hand, is a radical shift. "I know myself by my intentions. I know others by my interpretations." I know you by the stories I *make up* about what I believe your words and actions *really* mean. This leads to increased responsibility and to an empowering possibility. If I change my stories, I change my reaction. In other words, I create my own reactions. A subtle shift, but radically different than popular belief. "You made me angry!" Nope. "I interpreted your words and actions as an attack, as an attempt to thwart what I want, and my thoughts aroused anger within me." And if one is really objective they might add, "And frankly, there's a good chance I misunderstood what you meant to convey."

"I know you by my interpretations" is both a sobering and calming perspective. Rather than believing, defending, and reacting to your own interpretations, if you maintain awareness of the possibility of misunderstanding (an awareness that will have a grounding effect), you open the door to more rational relationships—you will calm yourself and put your thinking mind in charge.

Let's look at the interpersonal gap from yet another angle. To understand your own reactions and to convey useful feedback to another, it's important to be as clear as you can about what "action" you are interpreting. When you are conversing with someone, what sort of behavior are you taking in?

For our purposes, there are three primary sources of behavioral information: words, body language, and tone of voice. Words are what the person is saying and what you are hearing them say (which may be two different things!). Body language is constant and includes the powerful information conveyed by facial expression. Are they smiling? Frowning? Looking at you? Leaning toward you? Leaning back? Tensing their muscles? Slumped in their posture? Folding their arms? All body language provides information about the sender of the message, and is open to interpretation by the receiver. Last, but not necessarily least, does the tone of voice match the words being conveyed? Think of the various tones that could be used with the words "Thanks a lot." As you can probably surmise, very different messages can be conveyed, depending on the tone.

A famous study by Dr. Albert Mehrabian assessed where the receiver tuned in for understanding, when the messages from these three aspects of behavior (body, tone, and words) were inconsistent. Mehrabian's research breaks them down into percentages. What percentage do you think you get the message from when there are mixed messages from the sender? Take your best guess, and then see below:

Body language: _____%
Words: _____%
Tone: _____%

In Dr. Mehrabian's research, these were the percentages (Mehrabian, accessed through the public domain):

Body language: 55%
Tone: 38%
Words: 7%

If you answered differently, that doesn't invalidate your answer. You may be getting more of your information from one or two of these sources than did the people in the study, or you may be closer to the study's numbers than you realize. Either way, your ability to be specific about what you are reacting to will increase your own clarity about your reactions and improve the clarity of the feedback you give to others. For example, when you believe you are receiving a mixed message, you could think or say something like this: "When you said you were happy, you were frowning, so I didn't believe it." Compare that to somebody being affected by the same behavior, and thinking or saying, "liar." Feedback that primarily conveys specific behavior is generally less inflammatory than feedback that primarily or solely conveys judgments (interpretations). It's also more likely that the receiver and the sender can learn from and act on behaviorally specific feedback. The ability to give behaviorally specific feedback, free of interpretations, is essential if you are in a position of supervision, and important at home if you want less fighting and more understanding. Frankly, if you can't be behaviorally specific, you are better off not saying anything at all. How you put things and what you focus on does matter. (The topic of giving and receiving feedback is explored in more depth in Chapter 13 of *Leadership Can Be Learned.*)

You can also pay attention to the alignment of these three variables in your own communication. How aware are you of your own facial expressions? Do you smile when you are anxious or delivering a serious message? Many people smile because they are afraid of how the message will be received. Others cover their inner state by never varying their expression. Unfortunately, either behavior is likely to be confusing to the person on the receiving end. And neither behavior protects you from conveying *something*, sometimes conveying messages very different than what you intended. Ironically, people who have a more or less consistently blank facial expression, especially if they are in positions of authority, are often misinterpreted more, because people have less to go on and are filling in the blanks with their own imaginations (and with authority figures, they often imagine the worst).

If you want people to get a clear message, try smiling when you like what's happening, and looking serious when you feel serious. Family therapist Virginia Satir calls this match between your inner experience and your outer expression "congruency." As mentioned earlier, we all started life that way. When you were happy you looked happy, when you were sad you looked sad, and so on. If you have ever been around an infant, you know this to be true. From that point on, we all learned habits of what to show and what not to show. Through persistent intentional effort, you can unlearn those habits that are no longer serving you well, and relearn how to be congruent when you want to be.

The same is true of tone, and of words. As the Toltec Mayans have known for thousands of years, your words are powerful. Endeavor to say what you mean, and mean what you say. Be kind with your words, to yourself (in your head), and to others. Keep your word.

Wallen identified four ways to close interpersonal gaps. Read Appendix A (in *Leadership Can Be Learned*) and experiment with them. Remember, not every experiment will go the way you want it to. Learning new behaviors can be awkward, and the people you are with may not know what to make of your efforts. But just because you fall down doesn't mean learning to walk is a mistake. If the voice in your head starts being negative the first time you try new behavior and the interaction doesn't go the way you want, challenge that filter!

It might be with you the rest of your life, but you don't have to listen to it! Thank goodness that filter is a learned habit and wasn't in place when you were learning to walk and talk! You can stumble and still move forward. It doesn't mean that you, or the method, is a failure. Be clear about what you want, and go after it. The more you try on the behaviors in this book, the more you'll forge your own path, your own style, and create more of what you want at home and at work.

Appendix B
The PECO Nuclear Turnaround

This is a reprint from my book *Fight, Flight, Freeze: Emotional Intelligence, Behavioral Science, Systems Theory & Leadership.*

Peach Bottom Atomic Power Station

The following story of deep and successful culture change is written from a practitioner's point of view. Our hypothesis, that organizations that respect the role of emotion in human systems (in concert with other variables such as role, goal, and decision clarity) will meet or exceed their performance expectations was realized with dramatic fashion in this and numerous other scenarios. The methodology is a blueprint for culture change.

Research has consistently demonstrated that Emotional Intelligence is the critical variable in professional performance. This is especially true in a hierarchy, where authority relationships are prone to irrational behavior by both bosses and subordinates. Yet hierarchy has survived thousands of years because it is a fundamentally sound way to structure organizational relationships, by creating some simple clarity about authority and decision making.

Because hierarchical relationships are so easy to screw up, it has been a fad the past few decades to try to "fix" the problem by eliminating hierarchy. While there is in many cases value gained by reducing layers (along with undesired consequences, such as confusion, demoralization, and lost expertise, that are often underestimated and poorly managed), the   problem is not hierarchy. The problem is how humans manage positional authority (their dealings with the people above and below). Simply eliminating layers, or even worse, eliminating front line supervision does not "empower." More often than not, it creates chaos. The Uddevalla Volvo plant, touted in Tom Peter's Search for Excellence, is a prime example, opening with no frontline supervision (for which they drew acclaim) and closing for lack of productivity.

Whatever your structure, the challenge is how to manage authority for the good of the system, not whether to have it in the system. Drawing on our research and experience within and outside of the US nuclear industry, it is impossible to ignore the importance of how people manage authority relationships. If hierarchical relationships are managed in a rational manner, i.e., one that recognizes the importance of emotion and encourages an open flow of information, then Operational Experience (OE) (as the sharing of incidents and best practices is known in the nuclear industry) and other programmatic approaches to culture, including nuclear safety culture, simply enhance an already robust system. If hierarchical relationships are handled irrationally, then programmatic attempts at safety culture will result in little more than a Band-Aid on a dysfunctional system. Emotionally intelligent leadership and high performance culture are mirror images of each other, can be reliably developed, and are directly related to all aspects of human performance.

In 1987 the Nuclear Regulatory Commission (NRC) shutdown Peach Bottom Atomic Station (PBAPS) due to human performance issues. When the Philadelphia Electric Company (PECO) began rebuilding their Nuclear organization, they happened upon my father, Robert P. Crosby, one of a legion of resources brought to bear on the organization. Crosby began applying the same techniques he had been honing since the 1950s. His prior experience with DOE and Rancho Seco Nuclear helped open the door. At Rancho Seco he crafted a turnaround on the motor operated valve project that was months behind schedule (unfortunately, that effort and additional culture change work was wasted when the public voted to shut down the site permanently). At PECO, Crosby emerged as the leader of the extensive Organization Development (OD) activity that took place in the wake of the shutdown. This paper explores his culture change methods, including the role of experiential learning to enhance Emotional Intelligence and complementary elements of self-awareness, which he and his associates have replicated in numerous organizations and continue to utilize today.

On March 31, 1987, Peach Bottom Atomic Power Station was indefinitely shut down, following a series of human performance and equipment related incidents. Infamously, operators were found sleeping on the job, playing video games, engaging in rubber band and paper ball fights, and reading unauthorized material.

As if in anticipation of the Institute of Nuclear Power Operators (INPO) yet to be developed human performance model, blame was not simply placed on the operators. "Latent organizational weakness" was targeted by industry experts and regulators alike. INPO President Zack Pate came to the unprecedented conclusion that, "Major changes in the corporate culture at PECO are required." In September of 1988 NRC Chairman Lando Zech told senior management officials of PECO, "Your operators certainly made mistakes, no question about that. Your corporate management problems are just as serious." Clearly a culture characterized by low morale and apathy prevailed. By April 1988 this unusual emphasis on mismanagement contributed to the President of PECO resigning and the retirement of the CEO.

By 1996 both Limerick and Peach Bottom were designated excellent by INPO, and given strong Systematic Assessment of Licensee Performance (SALP) ratings by the NRC. Many factors contributed to this stunning success story. The following are the key organization development strategies that were employed:

1. Clarify Goals and Cascade Alignment

Management must lead and communicate. They must set clear measurable goals, such as increased capacity factor (a measure of how much electricity a generator produces relative to the maximum it could produce during the same period) and lower costs, and lead towards them. They must continually communicate the goals, and engage the organization to understand, monitor, and support efforts to achieve the goals. Equally important, they must stay in touch so as to understand and clear up any misunderstanding regarding the direction they have set.

Crosby understood that alignment must be built layer by layer, and that "you can only truly sponsor your direct reports." Innumerable change efforts have crashed and burned due to failure to understand this principle. Skip a layer and you create a black hole, sucking the energy out of the initiative. When on top of their game, PECO Nuclear's leadership followed Crosby's adaptation of Daryl Conner's change model. Each layer of sustaining sponsorship was carefully brought on board and charged with the task of driving change to the next layer of the organization. Through cascading dialogue, each layer was positioned both to lead and sustain the current goals of the organization.

PECO Nuclear's leadership cascaded clear and compelling goals time and again during and after the turn around. They did so early on by educating the organization about de-regulation and the increasingly competitive environment the industry was facing, by targeting outage length and the millions of dollars in lost revenue that the industry had accepted since its inception, and even after they had firmly established themselves as peak performers, by setting the bar even higher through bold initiatives such as "Mission Possible" and "Target 2000." Mission Possible was a masterpiece of combining a clear and serious message with playfulness, such as a video of the trench coat clad President of PECO Nuclear accepting a self-destructing tape from the CEO with the organization's new mission "should he choose to accept it." Such creativity, coupled with an unrelenting drive towards excellence, characterized the PECO Nuclear story.

2. Develop a Critical Mass of Employees with High Interactive Skills

Setting clear goals without developing the organization is as likely to backfire as not. General Burnside, during the American Civil War, set clear goals at Fredericksburg, ignored the "feedback" he got from his subordinates, and stood firm while thousands charged needlessly and fruitlessly to their deaths. The US Nuclear Industry has its own examples, such as The Clinton Significant Event Report (SER), which pointed out that the pursuit of production goals was actually part of the problem leading to the 1996 incident at that station. The SER cites management emphasis on the need to "maximize plant capacity factors and minimize forced outage rate" as an underlying cause ... goals which are shared by every nuclear plant in the nation.

Such goals need to be balanced with a carefully reinforced emphasis on conservative decision making and surfacing of issues. A culture of openness must be fostered or vital information will stay underground. To this end, a critical mass of employees at all levels of the organization must work on managing authority relationships with a high degree of maturity. This learning must be experiential and not just standard classroom, and be reinforced in subsequent live work interactions.

Crosby helped foster such a culture through all of his interventions, but especially through a week-long experiential learning workshop referred to at PECO Nuclear as Conflict Management. The emerging leadership of the organization almost universally attended, as did a vast majority of the workforce, often with layers, functions, and even locations mixed together to achieve a unique team building. Based on the principles of Social Scientist Kurt Lewin, who stands to a significant degree as the founder of organization development, the Crosby trainings (as they were also often called) utilized the power of group learning.

The primary methodology was a modified T-group, which when led by Crosby and/or his associates, focuses the participants on immediate behavior change and emotional intelligence to a degree that cannot be matched through individual coaching or traditional classroom learning. The result was a widely spread behavioral skill set including an increased capacity to foster a productive nuclear safety environment by giving clear direction, taking a stand for what you believe in, holding yourself and others accountable, fostering communication up and down the hierarchy, managing conflict, connecting with emotional intelligence to all levels of the organization, and continually developing yourself, others, and the organization. As one early participant put it (who later rose to the level of VP of Peach Bottom Atomic Power Station), "before conflict management we thought we were open, but the real meetings would happen after the meeting. People talked about each other and pointed fingers. After conflict management we started dealing with each other much more directly. At times it is difficult, but it is much more productive."

At the core of such learning is the assertion that hierarchical relationships are emotional, that the emotional tone of the organization is a key variable in human performance, and that a mature and rational approach to emotionality is an essential foundation for sustained performance. An explosion of research supports the assertion that the critical factor in career success is not IQ, but rather EQ, otherwise known as Emotional Intelligence. While high IQ can be a blessing, it can also be a curse if coupled with an inability to connect with others and turn one's ideas into action. For ages, people have unwittingly pursued this curse, trying to control their emotions by denying or ignoring them. Ironically, such an attempt is based on fear of emotion, and hence is irrational. Worse, it blinds the individual to the data available from their own inner guidance system. If blind to emotion, one is more likely to act off it without understanding the root cause of their action. To be rational about one's emotions, one must use their cognitive brain to pay attention to the messages that emotion is providing. Fortunately, science is proving that by working on awareness of emotion in yourself and in others, you don't have to be an Einstein to increase your emotional maturity, which in turn is a major determinate of success and happiness. Again, as Daniel Goleman pointed out in *Working with Emotional Intelligence*:

- ■ EQ accounted for 67% of the abilities deemed necessary for superior performance
- ■ EQ mattered TWICE as much as technical expertise or IQ

Although the process of working on EQ and other behavioral skills through Conflict Management was an alien experience for most, the results spoke for themselves, and helped reinforce strong sponsorship for the process. The process was even applied in 1999 to the new operator's class at Peach Bottom. The prior class had been marked by conflict between the operators and the instructors, as well as low marks by the NRC for teamwork and leadership. The class that incorporated the conflict management process passed with flying colors. The following is a scale of interactive skills from Robert P. Crosby's second organization development book, *The Cross-Functional Workplace*. These same behavioral traits were reinforced at every level of PECO Nuclear through experiential learning:

Leader's Interactive Skill Scale

	Stage	Description of Level	Inner Beliefs & Perceptions of Reality
High	+6	Empathic connection with others, yet still decisive	"I can walk in your moccasins and be myself which includes being decisive."
	+5	Is clear about wants	"I'll tell you what I need in order to succeed."
	+4	Acknowledgement of one's own part in the Interaction	"I help create the dance."
Medium	+3	Non-blaming; is specific about behavior and emotions	"Telling it straight is to give non-interpretive feedback."
	+2	Blaming, but is behaviorally specific	"Naming your behaviors proves my judgement."
	+1	Inner awareness, but manifest in blaming	"My judgements are the truth about you."
Low	0	Inner awareness, but non-communicative	"If I stay quiet, things will be 'cool.'"
	-1	Inner awareness, but outward distortion	"Telling the truth will make it worse."
	-2	Unaware, with 'cool' blaming	"Let reason conquer emotions."

Figure B.1

Leaders interactive skill scale

Such learning is important throughout an organization. It's vitally important that people manage their relationships with their positional superiors as rationally as possible. The goal is for as many as possible to take responsibility for relating to their boss about the support and resources they need in order to get their jobs done. Ultimately though there is no more emotionally loaded role than that of "boss." A critical mass of leaders working to encourage open communication from subordinates, and truly getting the emotional impact they have due to their role, is the essential foundation for high performance. React defensively, and/or with blame, and only the boldest subordinate will continue telling you what they really think. With this in mind, encouraging critical feedback and pursuing clarity in such a moment ("please tell me more— what precisely did I do or say that led you to that conclusion?") is a key focus in the Crosby experiential learning process.

In short, PECO Nuclear had learned through painful experience that without intentional on-going people development, communication withers and complacency results. This is especially true of successful organizations. All individuals and organizations have blind spots. As the Clinton VP put it, "We believe complacency played an important part in our performance decline. We thought we had established all the programs and practices necessary to be a top performing plant."

3. Reinforce Goal Alignment and Continuous Improvement Conversations in All Intact Teams

After an initial period of experimentation, PECO Nuclear adapted an increasingly standardized expectation that every team stop periodically to assess how it's functioning. Bosses and subordinates participated at least annually in a live facilitated upward, downward and peer feedback session, and the entire group strategized on how to improve their work within the context of the organization's goals. Facilitation helped assure active listening, and helped target coaches to those groups and supervisors most in need. Behavioral skill building was built into the process.

This strategy of work group continuous improvement was sustained for years at PECO Nuclear through a unique survey-feedback process, and through New Reporting Relationship (NRR) meetings, based on a model originally developed by the US Navy. The survey process allowed each intact work group to see their own data, derive their own conclusions, and develop solutions to problems within their own sphere of influence. The NRR meetings occurred at all levels. They served the dual purpose of supporting a smooth transition whenever a leadership change occurred, and of seizing continuous improvement opportunities during the change.

Coupled with the other OD interventions, each team session drove the following systemic characteristics. See Figure B.2 on the opposite page (again excerpted from *The Cross-Functional Workplace*).

4. Drive Cultural Change through Key Cross-Functional Projects.

A classic example of this occurred during Crosby's support at PECO Nuclear as they changed their approach to outages. At the time the industry norm was 70 days to refuel a nuclear plant. Each plant lost somewhere in the vicinity of a million dollars a day in lost revenue. The potential payoff was obvious and huge, but the fear of decreasing the quality of workmanship was understandable and strong. Based on experience in a prior nuclear plant, Crosby was convinced the issue was organizational and behavioral, not some mythical requirement of a certain length to assure quality. Working with and coaching a hard driving leader, he helped Limerick

Dimension	Unhealthy System	Healthy System
Management	Frantic	Centered
Influence	None	Appropriate
Alignment	Not well aligned	Well aligned
Communication	Gossip—closed	Openness and dialogue
Consequence management	Capricious discipline	Clear consequence
Decision-making	Consistently extreme (either consensual or authoritarian)	Flexible and clear
Interactive Skill	Low	High
Task Goals	Unclear	Clear
Accountability	Fuzzy	Single-point
Implementation	Poor	Effective
Rewards	None	Appropriate
Sponsorship	Poor	Clear

Figure B.2

Characteristics of healthy and unhealthy systems

Generating Station organize their outage cross-functionally, and instill the behaviors, including basics such as working to and adhering to a clear timeline, resulting in a more organized effort. PECO's leadership seized the model, and set a string of record length short outages coupled with equally unprecedented problem free operating runs.

In the Crosby culture change model (influenced by his early years as a community organizer) *change doesn't come if the effort is limited to trainings (although training can support change).* Crosby helped change the organization by implementing desired behaviors in the context of key initiatives. Outage execution, for example, is an excellent time to reinforce single point accountability, conservative decision making, conflict resolution skills, surfacing of issues, and related behaviors. The organization becomes the classroom, with each layer responsible for continuous improvement by rapidly surfacing issues (such as the possibility of missing a deadline), and by giving and receiving behavioral feedback.

Such efforts include participative large group planning processes with a cross-section of the organization including the hourly workforce. Again, Crosby's methods build the larger team while focusing on a business critical task. His blend of community organizing and organization development improves the quality of the output (planning that includes the people who execute the plan is almost guaranteed to be a better product), increasing ownership, immediate word-of-mouth communication, and most importantly, successful implementation. The same methods have been applied to many organizations outside the industry, in pursuit of key goals such as increased capacity, or reduced costs, with reliable results.

5. Create a "Cadre" of Key Line People Early in the Process Who Can Help Facilitate the Change.

Cadre played a key role at PECO Nuclear, assisting in the change process, decreasing the organization's reliance on external resources, and continuing to develop the organization from within. These people, recruited from the hourly as well as the management ranks, were equipped with above all else high interactive skills fostered through the Conflict Management workshops and additional training. Aside from their role in facilitating change, many cadre members rose through the ranks in the organization, to as high as the Nuclear Group President.

At Peach Bottom, they were woven into every initiative, and provided the following on a formal and informal basis:

- Individual coaching regarding conflict, communication skills, etc.
- Third party conflict resolution
- Meeting design and/or facilitation
- Survey feedback and NRR facilitation

Cadre members were woven into key initiatives and many rose to the highest ranks of the organization.

Conclusion: In short, the transformation of PECO Nuclear was no fluke. Many variables came together, including great personnel and a unique burning platform. Nonetheless, the organization development approach described above was a best practice and critical enabler, transforming the organization from a rigid and de-motivating hierarchy to an empowered culture built on a clear and thoughtful balance between management authority and employee influence. Leaders both formal and informal at every level learned how to take clear stands and stay connected. The same methods are reliable and reproducible, and continue to be implemented in nuclear and non-nuclear organizations to this day.

Appendix C
KRID (Adapt/Adopt)
(Successfully Sharing Best Practices)

Reprinted with permission from *Strategic Engagement: Practice Tools to Raise Morale and Increase Results Volume II: System-Wide Activities* by Chris Crosby.

Most workplaces use best practices from other workgroups or organizations. Sometimes sharing a best practice has the unintended consequences of creating employees who instead of learning and adapting a new process, resist the new ideas entirely. This appendix will help you effectively share knowledge and best practices in various settings. Although specifically related to best practices, it is also a great way to recap large events where multiple workgroups have had similar experiences, such as the cascading of goal alignment (Chapter 3 of *Volume II*) or survey feedback (Chapter 4 of *Volume I*).

History: When, in the 1950s, Dr. Spencer Havilik experienced the City of Milwaukee shelve his water study (which, we now know, would have saved the city 100s of millions), it was for him the last straw. He found Dr. Ronald Lippitt at the Institute for Social Research, University of Michigan, and with others they founded the Center for Research in the Utilization of Scientific Knowledge (CRUSK).

Goal: To research the miss or unuse of knowledge, resistance to the same, and develop methodologies to effectively connect expertise (including research, theory, and successful practice knowledge) to practitioners/appliers who face problems/possibilities that could be enriched by the knowledge.

From this history and the nearly 30-year mentorship with Dr. Ronald Lippitt, Robert P. Crosby developed a step-by-step technique to successfully share best practices. KRID stands for Knowledge Retrieval Implication Derivation.

Here is a short lead-in to the process.

Most employees can remember a new program imposed by management, insisting that everyone follow the same practice. Many can also remember initiatives (quality initiatives, new business systems) that failed. These failed attempts are called "fads" or "flavor-of-the-month" programs. Why do they fail and what creates success in disseminating good practices so that results are achieved? First, let's review two extremes that guarantee failure.

Become a true believer in the practice and push it on everyone. This is the most popular implementation method. Companies spend mega-bucks on "cookie-cutter" approaches, and training companies flourish by marketing such packages. CEOs often forget the wisdom about managing for results, not for "activities." They count activities—how many people attend quality training or how many crews are now "self-directed" —rather than checking if such trainings or new practices are producing better results in productivity, safety, cost, and quality.

In this extreme, experts on the particular methodology or program being implemented are dispatched to convince, coerce, or otherwise manipulate the resisting parties to conform to the new approach. Consequently, even if the top executive mandated the change, intense resistance and sabotage of the essentials still occur in the new method.

Let the employees decide if they want to adopt the new program. In the other failure scenario, the new practice is suggested and left for individual or group discretion. A few adopt it, some adapt it to fit their needs, and many ignore it.

There is a better way. The key difference is between the words "adopt" and "adapt"—

Adopt = Swallow it whole

Adapt = Fit it to your needs

- and in the paradoxical blending of these two in a unified construct.

Apply these fundamental principles and steps when sharing successful practices.

1. The successful practice must be presented, warts and all, as it is practiced. Presenters of this knowledge must not a) generalize to other situations, b) attempt to apply it for the audience, nor c) sell it. Rather, they must share accurate data with genuine enthusiasm but no exhortations ("This is the greatest thing since sliced bread!") or admonitions ("You must do this or lose market share!").

2. As clearly as possible, measurable outcomes—for which all will be accountable—must be identified and communicated by the sponsoring executives. People will be held accountable for successful results rather than replicating the method.

3. Those receiving the knowledge about the successful practice must demonstrate their ability to accurately articulate the original practice. No arguing. Rather, repeat the words and paraphrase the meanings (i.e., "Here is what I heard you say, and I'm translating it into the following meanings. Do my meanings match your message?").

4. The receivers derive implications for their unique situation. Temporarily accepting the validity of the successful practice, they consider how to implement the process to fit their environment.

5. The initiating executive or key manager, perhaps in the midst of step four, clarifies those aspects, if any, of the practice that are so central that they are not negotiable. Thus, the

receivers are clear about what must be *adopted* and what can be *adapted*. While striving for results and not activities as the goal, the executive may have compelling reasons (e.g., standardizing purchasing of costly equipment) to "edict" certain core elements. That which is to be adopted will be met by resistance, of course, which leads to the next step.

6. The initiating executive must listen, stay firm about the core, respect disagreement, and respect anger or frustration if it surfaces. After appropriate airing, they should restate the core (which may have shifted slightly—but genuinely, not as the result of placating but of careful listening) and then the firm expectation that people will follow the leader!

7. Work completion includes selecting and sequencing the practices to adapt, and planning additional training or resources to implement the adopted and adapted practices.

Successful knowledge transfer is enhanced by understanding the adoption/adaptation distinction. One should minimize adoption and maximize adaptation while focusing on results instead of methods. Adaptation is a natural process because 1) situations to implement new practices are unique, 2) communicating a complex practice is likely to have misunderstandings, 3) humans are motivated most when using their own creative juices, and 4) success increases with involvement and belief in the process by those who will complete the practice daily.

Conclusion

KRID remains one of the most practical and powerful ways to share knowledge in any organization that struggles with using learnings from internal or external sources. The process is simple to learn and can be adapted to serve your needs any time. Learn its foundations and add it to your tool kit.

Bibliography

Aasland, S., Skogstad, A., Notelaers, G., Nielsen, M. and Einarsen, S. (2009). *The Prevalence of Destructive Leadership Behaviour.* British Journal of Management, Vol. 21. Oxford, UK. British Academy of Management.

Benne, K. (1976). *The Processes of Re-Education: An Assessment of Kurt Lewin's Views.* Group & Organization Studies, March 1976,1(1), 26-42. University Associates, Inc.

Bennis, W. (2010). *Still Surprised.* San Francisco, CA: Jossey-Bass.

Bennis, W., Benne, K. and Chin, R. (1961). *The Planning of Change.* New York, NY. Holt, Rinehart and Winston, Inc.

Bradford, L., Gibb, J. and Benne, K. (1964). *T-Group Theory & Laboratory Method: Innovation in Re-education.* New York, NY. John Wiley & Sons, Inc.

Bridgman, T., Brown, K. and Cummings, S. (2016). *Unfreezing Change as Three Steps: Rethinking Kurt Lewin's Legacy for Change Management.* Human Relations. Vol. 69(1) 33–60. Sage Publications.

Burnes, B. (2019). *The Role of Alfred J. Marrow and the Harwood Manufacturing Corporation in the Advancement of OD.* The Journal of Applied Behavioral Science. Vol. 55(4) 397-427. Sage Publications.

Burnes, B. and Cooke, B. (2012). *The Past, Present and Future of Organization Development: Taking the Long View.* United Kingdom. Human Relations. Sage Publications.

Coates, R., Ferber, A. and Brunsma, D. (2018). *The Matrix of Race: Social Construction, Intersectionality, and Inequality.* United Kingdom. SAGE Publications.

Coates, R. (2018). Personal correspondence.

Crosby, C. (2019). *Strategic Engagement: Practice Tools to Raise Morale and Increase Results Volume I: Core Activities*. New York, NY. Business Expert Press LLC.

Crosby, C. (2019). *Strategic Engagement: Practice Tools to Raise Morale and Increase Results Volume II: System-Wide Activities*. New York, NY. Business Expert Press LLC.

Crosby, G. (2008). *Fight, Flight, Freeze: Emotional Intelligence, Behavioral Science, Systems Theory & Leadership*. Seattle, WA. CrosbyOD Publishing.

Crosby, G. (2019). *In Defense of Lewin: Planned Change for the Ages*. OD Review. Volume 51, Number 4. OD Network.

Crosby, G. (2018). *Leadership Can Be Learned: Clarity, Connection, and Results*. Boca Raton, FL. Taylor & Francis Group.

Crosby, G. (2018). *T-Groups as a Catalyst for Individual, Group and Organizational Change*. OD Practitioner. Volume 50, Number 3. OD Network.

Crosby, R. (2011). *Cultural Change in Organizations: A Guide to Leadership and Bottom-Line Results*. Seattle, WA. CrosbyOD Publishing.

Crosby, R. (2019). *Memoirs of a Change Agent: T-groups, Organization Development, and Social Justice*. Seattle, WA. CrosbyOD Publishing.

Crosby, R. (2015). *The Cross-Functional Workplace*. Seattle, WA. CrosbyOD Publishing.

Crosby, R (1992). *Walking the Empowerment Tightrope: Balancing Management Authority & Employee Influence*. King of Prussia, PA. HRDQ.

Ferris, K. (2019). *Change Management's Dirty Little Secret*. Published on LinkedIn.

Friedman, E. (1999). *A Failure of Nerve: Leadership in the Age of the Quick Fix.* New York, NY. Seabury Books.

Friedman, E. (1985). *Generation to Generation: Family Process in Church and Synagogue.* New York, NY. The Guilford Press.

Grabbe, P., Lewin, K. (1945). *Conduct, Knowledge and Acceptance of New Values.* Journal of Social Issues. No 1.

Human Relations Raises Sales 300%. (1948, February 16). The New York Times, p. 31.

Kleiner, A. (1996). *The Age of Heretics: A History of the Radical Thinkers Who Reinvented Corporate Management.* San Francisco, CA. Jossey-Bass.

Kohn, R. *Eagle and Sword: The Federalists and the Creation of the Military Establishment in America, 1783-1802.* New York, NY. Free Press.

Lewin, K. (1946). *Action Research and Minority Problems.* Journal of Social Issues. No 2.

Lewin, K. (1946). *Behavior and Development as a Function of the Total Situation.* Manual of Child Psychology. New York, NY. John Wiley & Sons.

Lewin, K. (1940). *Bringing Up the Jewish Child.* The Menorah Journal. Volume 28, No 1.

Lewin, K. (1943). *Cultural Reconstruction.* Journal of Abnormal and Social Psychology. No 38.

Lewin, K. (1943). *Defining the Field at a Given Time.* Psychology Review. Volume 50, No 3.

Lewin, G. and Lewin, K. (1941). *Democracy and the School.* Understanding the Child. Volume 10.

Lewin, K. (1939). *Experiments in Social Space.* Harvard Educational Review. Volume 9, No 1.

Lewin, K. (1938). *Experiments on Autocratic and Democratic Atmospheres.* The Social Frontier. Volume 4, No 37.

Lewin, K. (1942). *Field Theory and Learning.* Yearbook of National Social Studies Education. Volume 41, Part 2.

Lewin, K. (1940). *Formalization and Progress in Psychology.* University of Iowa Studies in Child Welfare. University of Iowa. Volume 16, No 3.

Lewin, K. (1947). *Frontiers in Group Dynamics.* Human Relations. London. Tavistock Institute.

Lewin, K. (1948). *Group Decision and Social Change.* Readings in Social Psychology. New York, NY. Henry Holt.

Lewin, K. (1944). *Jewish Education and Reality.* Jewish Education. Volume 15, No 3.

Lewin, K., Lippitt, R. and White, R. (1939). *Patterns of Aggressive Behavior in Experimentally Created "Social Climates".* Journal of Social Psychology. No 10.

Lewin, K. (1941). *Personal Adjustment and Group Belongingness.* The Jewish Social Service Quarterly. No 17.

Lewin, K. (1936). *Principles of Topological Psychology.* New York, NY. McGraw-Hill.

Lewin, K. (1943). *Psychology and the Process of Group Living.* The Journal of Social Psychology. SPSSI Bulletin. No 17.

Lewin, K. (1943). *Psychological Ecology.* University of Iowa Studies in Child Welfare. University of Iowa.

Lewin, K. (1935). *Psycho-Sociological Problems of a Minority Group.* Character and Personality. No 3.

Lewin, K. (1941). *Regression, Retrogression, and Development.* University of Iowa Studies in Child Welfare. Volumn 18, No 1.

Lewin, K. (1997). *Resolving Social Conflicts & Field Theory in Social Science.* Washington DC. American Psychological Association.

Lewin, K. (1936). *Some Social-Psychological Differences Between the United States and Germany.* Character and Personality. Volume 4.

Lewin, K. (1940). *The Background of Conflict in Marriage.* Modern Marriage. New York, NY. S.S. Cross.

Lewin, K. (1999). *The Complete Social Scientist.* Washington DC. American Psychological Association.

Lewin, K. (1944). *The Dynamics of Group Action.* Educational Leadership. No 4.

Lewin, K. (1944). *The Solution of a Chronic Conflict in Industry.* Proceedings of the Second Brief Psychotherapy Council. Chicago, IL. Institute for Psychoanalysis.

Lewin, K. (1943). *The Special Case of Germany.* Public Opinion Quarterly. No 7.

Lewin, K. (1942). *Time Perspective and Morale.* Civilian Morale. Second Yearbook of the SPSSI. Boston. Reynal & Hitchcock by Houghton Mifflin.

Lewin, K. (1939). *When Facing Danger.* Jewish Frontier.

Likert, R. (1947). *Kurt Lewin: A Pioneer in Human Relations Research.* Ann Arbor, MI, University of Michigan.

Lippitt, R. and White, R. (1960). *Autocracy and Democracy: An Experimental Inquiry.* New York, NY. Harper & Brothers.

Lippitt, R., Watson, J. and Westley, B. (1958). *The Dynamics of Planned Change.* New York, NY. Harcourt, Brace & World.

Lippitt, R. (1949). *Training in Community Relations.* New York, NY. Harper Brothers.

Marrow, A., (1969). *The Practical Theorist: The Life and Work of Kurt Lewin.* New York, NY. Teacher's College Press.

Mehrabian, A. (1981). *Silent Messages.* Belmont, CA. Wadsworth.

Ruiz, D.M. (1997). *The Four Agreements*. San Rafael, CA. Amber Allen Publishing.

Satir, V. (1972). *People Making*. Palo Alto, CA. Science and Behavior Books.

Schein, E. (1987). *Process Consultation Volume II: Lessons for Managers and Consultants*. Reading, MA. Addison-Wesley Publishing Company.

Schmuck, R. (2006). *Practical Action Research for Change*. Thousand Oaks, CA. Corwin Press, Inc.

Thurman, H. (1949). *Jesus and the Disinherited*. Boston, MA. Beacon Press.

Wallen, J. *The Interpersonal Gap*. Unpublished.

Welcome All Races, All Creeds, Minister Urges. (1962, February). Wausau Daily Herald, p1.

Winston, A. (1996). *Journal of the History of the Behavioral Sciences*. Volume 32.

Index

Printed in the United States
By Bookmasters